SECRETS
OF
AMERICAN
HISTORY

pil

Publications International, Ltd.

Written by Lisa Brooks, Julie Clark-Robinson, Ian Feigle, Martin Graham, Peter Haugen, Richard Mueller, Robert Norris, David Priess, Lawrence Robinson, Paul Seaburn, Lexi M. Schuh, and Peter Suciu

Images from Getty, Shutterstock.com, and Wikimedia Commons
Endsheet image provided by Eric Guikema

Louis Weber, CEO
Publications International, Ltd.
8140 Lehigh Avenue
Morton Grove, IL 60053

ISBN: 978-1-64558-393-6

Manufactured in China.

8 7 6 5 4 3 2 1

Table of Contents

Today, the world seems to be divided into two camps. One camp believes there are secret groups of powerful oligarchs controlling shadow governments in some grand plot to take over the world. And the other camp who views governments as completely incompetent, trusting little in the government's ability to govern their populaces effectively. No matter which way you look at it, the fact remains: the government—whether effective or not—is trying to cover its tracks. Either it doesn't want you to know how it's "pulling all the strings," or it doesn't want you to know how ineffective and confused it is. Secrets abound no matter your viewpoint.

Secrets of American History covers many of the American government's most controversial foibles, cover ups, and military operations. Some events are honest mistakes, and other events are actually conspiracies with malicious intent. CIA agents run amok with no accountability during the Red Scare. Objects and people appear and disappear mysteriously. Facts dissipate into the ether, and rumors abound. And those in power take action against the perceived threats toward American normalcy.

We'd be shocked if we really knew what happened behind the closed doors of our government buildings. We'd be horrified if we uncovered the scandals American institutions have carried out in the name of freedon and liberty. We may never know what type of operations are being conducted behind the security gates of our military bases, but we have plenty of clues pointing their way toward the truth. And *Secrets of American History* is here to point you in the right direction, explaining some of the nation's deepest secrets that have yet to be reckoned with.

Chapter 1

Political Scandals & Declassified Operations

Teapot Dome Scandal

The Teapot Dome Scandal was the largest of numerous scandals during the presidency of Warren Harding. Teapot Dome is an oil field reserved for emergency use by the U.S. Navy located on public land in Wyoming. Oil companies and politicians claimed the reserves were not necessary and that the oil companies could supply the Navy in the event of shortages. In 1922, Interior Secretary Albert B. Fall accepted $404,000 in illegal gifts from oil company executives in return for leasing the rights to the oil at Teapot Dome to Mammoth Oil without asking for competitive bids. The leases were legal but the gifts were not. Fall's attempts to keep the gifts secret failed, and, on April 14, 1922, *The Wall Street Journal* exposed the bribes. Fall denied the charges, but an investigation revealed a $100,000 no-interest loan in return for leases that Fall had forgotten to cover up. In 1927, the Supreme Court ruled that the oil leases had been illegally obtained, and the U.S. Navy regained control of Teapot Dome and other reserves. Fall was found guilty of bribery in 1929, fined $100,000, and sentenced to one year in prison. He was the first cabinet member imprisoned for his actions while in office. President Harding was not aware of the scandal at the time of his death in 1923, but it contributed to his administration being considered one of the most corrupt in history.

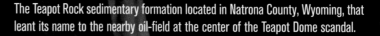
The Teapot Rock sedimentary formation located in Natrona County, Wyoming, that leant its name to the nearby oil-field at the center of the Teapot Dome scandal.

Top: A photo of Albert B. Fall, who was sentenced to jail for accepting bribes. He was the first U.S. cabinet member in the history of the U.S. to be sentenced to prison.

Bottom: A photo of the pumpjacks located near Teapot Dome, Wyoming.

Watergate

atergate is the name of the scandal that caused Richard Nixon to become the only U.S. president to resign from office. On May 27, 1972, concerned that Nixon's bid for reelection was in jeopardy, former CIA agent E. Howard Hunt, Jr., former New York assistant district attorney G. Gordon Liddy, former CIA operative James W. McCord, Jr., and six other men broke into the Democratic headquarters in the Watergate Hotel in Washington, D.C. They wiretapped phones, stole some documents, and photographed others. When they broke in again on June 17 to fix a bug that wasn't working, a suspicious security guard called the Washington police, who arrested McCord and four other burglars. A cover-up began to destroy incriminating evidence, obstruct investigations, and halt any spread of scandal that might lead to the president. On August 29, Nixon announced that the break-in had been investigated and that no one in the White House was involved. Despite his efforts to hide his involvement, Nixon was done in by his own tape recordings, one of which revealed that he had authorized hush money paid to Hunt. To avoid impeachment, Nixon resigned on August 9, 1974. His successor, President Gerald Ford, granted him a blanket pardon on September 8, 1974, eliminating any possibility that Nixon would be indicted and tried. *Washington Post* reporters Bob Woodward and Carl Bernstein helped expose the scandal using information leaked by someone identified as Deep Throat, a source whose identity was kept hidden until 2005, when it was revealed that Deep Throat was former Nixon administration member William Mark Felt.

Richard Nixon leaving the White House shortly before his resignation on August 9, 1974.

THE WHITE HOUSE

WASHINGTON

August 9, 1974

Dear Mr. Secretary:

I hereby resign the Office of President of the United States.

Sincerely,

Richard Nixon

11.35 AM

HK

The Honorable Henry A. Kissinger
The Secretary of State
Washington, D.C. 20520

Nixon's letter of resignation. Vice President Gerald Ford officially became president when Secretary of State Henry Kissinger initialed and timestamped the letter.

Gerald Ford signing the Proclamation Granting Pardon for Richard Nixon on September 8, 1974

The Iran-Contra Affair

On July 8, 1985, President Ronald Reagan told the American Bar Association that Iran was part of a "confederation of terrorist states." He failed to mention that members of his administration were secretly planning to sell weapons to Iran to facilitate the release of U.S. hostages held in Lebanon by pro-Iranian terrorist group Hezbollah. Profits from the arms sales were secretly sent to Nicaragua to aid rebel forces, known as the contras, in their attempt to overthrow the country's democratically-elected government. The incident became known as the Iran-Contra Affair and was the biggest scandal of Reagan's administration. The weapons sale to Iran was authorized by Robert McFarlane, head of the National Security Council (NSC), in violation of U.S. government policies regarding terrorists and military aid to Iran. NSC staff member Oliver North arranged for a portion of the $48 million paid by Iran to be sent to the contras, which violated a 1984 law banning this type of aid. North and his secretary Fawn Hall also shredded critical documents. President Reagan repeatedly denied rumors that the United States had exchanged arms for hostages, but later stated that he'd been misinformed. He created a Special Review Board to investigate. In February 1987, the board found the president not guilty. Others involved were found guilty but either had their sentences overturned on appeal or were later pardoned by George H. W. Bush.

Reagan listening to the findings of the Tower Commission Report, which held Reagan responsible for the affair due to his lax approach toward policy detail. The report also noted that the affair allowed the U.S. to simultaneously supply both Iran and Iraq with weapons during the Iran-Iraq War including constituents to make nerve gas, mustard gas, and chemical weapons.

Despite the embargo, President Reagan knew that Hawk surface-to-air and TOW anti-tank missiles were being sold to Iran.

Ronald and Nancy Reagan paying their respects to the victims of a Hezbollah attack on the American embassy in Beirut in 1983. Reagan's administration used Israel as a "middleman" to sell Ayatollah Khomeini's Islamic Republic of Iran arms in order to influence pro-Iranian terrorist group Hezbollah to release American hostages. The funds of the sale were then used to back the Contra rebel group in Nicaragua.

Truman's Revenue Scandal

President Harry Truman presided over some difficult times during our country's history: The atomic bomb era, the end of World War II, the "Red Scare," and the Korean War, just to name a few. In fact, Truman spent so much time dealing with significant issues that would later take up full chapters in history books that it's easy to forget that he was not immune to controversy. Like presidents before him and those who came after, Truman was also plagued by scandal.

In 1950, the Senate began investigating allegations of corruption among senior officials in the Truman administration. One of these officials was Truman's military aide, Harry Vaughn. The investigation discovered that Vaughn had been accepting bribes in return for political favors given to friends and businessmen. Perhaps the most interesting aspect of this discovery was the bribes themselves: Vaughn was given fur coats—and, strangely, deep freezers—from his associates. He gave one of these freezers to Bess Truman, but the appliances ended up being defective and the first lady's freezer broke within months. But defrosted freezer aside, Vaughn was found guilty of merely minor breeches of ethics. Truman stood beside his friend, pardoning the allegations, which some felt was an approval of Vaughn's actions.

President Truman and Brig. Gen. Harry Vaughan at the Gatow Airport in Berlin in July 1945.

But the most serious scandal during Truman's tenure went far beyond freezers. Back in 1913, when the Sixteenth Amendment to the Constitution was ratified–giving Congress permission to impose tax on income–the Bureau of Internal Revenue (now the IRS) was created. By 1950, rumors began to swirl that some people with serious tax problems were able to bypass trouble by paying bureau officials to look the other way. The allegations became so serious that Delaware Senator John J. Williams demanded an investigation, and between 1951 and 1952, Congress and the Treasury Department paid closer attention to IRS tax collectors.

Their investigation revealed a pattern of serious corruption within the IRS, with high-level officials often accepting favors and payments in return for ignoring tax violations and evasion. More than a hundred employees–166 in all–were either fired or resigned due to the scrutiny. But Attorney General J. Howard McGrath thought that special prosecutor Newbold Morris was "too zealous" in his investigation, and subsequently fired him. This didn't sit well with Truman, who felt that rooting out the corruption was the best way to save his reputation with the public. So Truman dismissed McGrath and replaced him with James McGranery, whose vision more clearly aligned with Truman's.

Nevertheless, the Bureau scandal left a mark in the minds of the American people. Truman knew that the controversy, along with the ongoing and unpopular Korean War, were issues that would make a campaign for reelection an uphill battle. On March 29, 1952, he announced his decision to not run for reelection, throwing his support behind the Democratic nominee, Adlai Stevenson, and heavily criticizing his opponent, Dwight D. Eisenhower.

After Truman's decision to not run for reelection, Dwight D. Eisenhower, pictured above, would go on to win the presidency in the 1952 election, but this would not be the end of the Truman-era Bureau of Internal Revenue scandals. In 1956, two former Truman officials—Matthew J. Connelly and T. Lamar Caudle—were convicted of accepting bribes in exchange for helping a shoe distributer avoid prosecution for tax evasion. Both men were sentenced to six months in prison, but were later pardoned.

Major General Harry Vaughan was an associate of President Truman since World War I.

Today, more than a hundred years after it was formed, the IRS continues to create controversy and scandal, and taxpayers continue to search for ways—legal and illegal—to avoid the dreaded agency.

Operation MKULTRA

From the mid-1950s through at least the early 1970s, thousands of unwitting Americans and Canadians became part of a bizarre CIA research project codenamed MKULTRA. Participants were secretly "brainwashed"—drugged with LSD and other hallucinogens, subjected to electroconvulsive shock therapy, and manipulated with abusive mind-control techniques.

MKULTRA began in 1953 under the orders of CIA director Allen Dulles. The program, which was in direct violation of the human rights provisions of the Nuremberg Code that the United States helped establish after WWII, was developed in response to reports that U.S. prisoners of war in Korea were being subjected to Communist mind-control techniques.

CIA researchers hoped to find a "truth drug" that could be used on Soviet agents, as well as drugs that could be used against foreign leaders (one documented scheme involved an attempt in 1960 to dose Fidel Castro with LSD). They also aimed to develop means of mind control that would benefit U.S. intelligence, perhaps including the creation of drone-like operatives to carry out assassinations. As part of MKULTRA, the CIA investigated parapsychology and such phenomena as hypnosis, telepathy, precognition, photokinesis, and "remote viewing."

MKULTRA was headed by Dr. Sidney Gottlieb, a military psychiatrist and chemist known as the "Black Sorcerer," who specialized in concocting deadly poisons. More than 30 universities and scientific institutes took part in MKULTRA. LSD and other mind-altering drugs including heroin, mescaline, psilocybin, scopolamine, marijuana, and sodium pentothal were given to CIA employees, military personnel, and other government workers, often without the subjects' knowledge or prior consent. To broaden their subject pool, researchers targeted unsuspecting civilians, often those in vulnerable or socially compromising situations. Prison inmates, prostitutes, and mentally ill hospital patients were often used. In a project codenamed Operation Midnight Climax, the CIA set up brothels in several U.S. cities to lure men as unwitting test subjects. Rooms were equipped with cameras that filmed the experiments behind one-way mirrors. Some civilian subjects who consented to participation were used for more extreme experimentation. One group of volunteers in Kentucky was given LSD for more than 70 straight days.

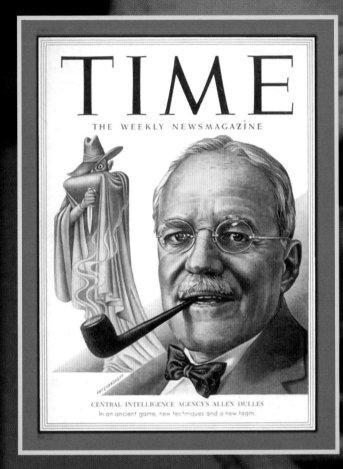

Operation MKULTRA began under the direction of CIA director Allen Dulles in 1953.

In the 1960s, Dr. Gottlieb also traveled to Vietnam and conducted mind-control experiments on Viet Cong prisoners of war being held by U.S. forces. During the same time period, an unknown number of Soviet agents died in U.S. custody in Europe after being given dual intravenous injections of barbiturates and amphetamine in the CIA's search for a truth serum.

MKULTRA experiments were also carried out in Montreal, Canada, between 1957 and 1964 by Dr. Donald Ewen Cameron, a researcher in Albany, New York, who also served as president of the World Psychiatric Association and the American and Canadian psychiatric associations. The CIA appears to have given him potentially deadly experiments to carry out at Canadian mental health institutes so U.S. citizens would not be involved. Cameron also experimented with paralytic drugs—in some cases inducing a coma in subjects for up to three months—as well as using electroconvulsive therapy at 30 times the normal voltage. The subjects were often women being treated for anxiety disorders and postpartum depression. Many suffered permanent damage. A lawsuit by victims of the experiments later uncovered that the Canadian government had also funded the project.

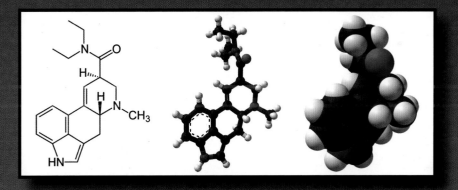

A diagram showing the skeletal, ball-and-stick, and space-filling models of lysergic acid diethylamide (LSD) molecule, a drug invented in 1938 by Swiss chemist Albert Hofmann.

Top: Many of the reports detailing the operations of MKULTRA were destroyed under the order of CIA director Richard Helms in 1973. Helms wanted to keep the operation under wraps due to the publicity the Watergate scandal had received. Investigations into MKULTRA did not begin until 1974 with the Church Committee and the Rockefeller Commission.

Right: Senator Frank Church, seen here in 1977 with President Carter, led the Church Committee investigation and found that the CIA had not obtained consent from the subjects of its experiments.

At least one American subject died in the experiments. Frank Olson, a U.S. Army biological weapons researcher, was secretly given LSD in 1953. A week later, he fell from a hotel window in New York City following a severe psychotic episode. A CIA doctor assigned to monitor Olson claimed he jumped from the window, but an autopsy performed on Olson's exhumed remains in 1994 found that he had been knocked unconscious before the fall.

The U.S. Army also conducted experiments with psychoactive drugs. A later investigation determined that nearly all Army experiments involved soldiers and civilians who had given their informed consent, and that Army researchers had largely followed scientific and safety protocols. Ken Kesey, who would later write *One Flew over the Cuckoo's Nest* and become one of the originators of the hippie movement, volunteered for LSD studies at an Army research center in San Francisco in 1960. LSD stolen from the Army lab by test subjects was some of the first in the world used "recreationally" by civilians. The Army's high ethical standards, however, seem to have been absent in at least one case. Harold Blauer, a professional tennis player in New York City who was hospitalized for depression following his divorce, died from apparent cardiac arrest during an Army experiment in 1952. Blauer had been secretly injected with massive doses of mescaline.

CIA researchers eventually concluded that the effects of LSD were too unpredictable to be useful, and the agency later acknowledged that their experiments made little scientific sense. Records on 150 MKULTRA research projects were destroyed in 1973 by order of CIA Director Richard Helms. A year later, *The New York Times* first reported about CIA experiments on U.S. citizens. In 1975, congressional hearings and a report by the Rockefeller Commission revealed details of the program. In 1976, President Gerald Ford issued an executive order prohibiting experimentation with drugs on human subjects without their informed consent. Ford and CIA Director William Colby also publicly apologized to Frank Olson's family, who received $750,000 by a special act of Congress.

Though no evidence exists that the CIA succeeded in its quest to find mind-control techniques, some conspiracy theories claim that the MKULTRA project was linked to the assassination of Robert F. Kennedy. Some have argued that Kennedy's assassin, Sirhan B. Sirhan, had been subjected to mind control. Sirhan claims that he has no recollection of shooting Kennedy, despite attempts by both government prosecutors and his defense lawyers to use hypnosis to recover his memories.

Former CIA operative, Frank Olson (above), died after he presumably threw himself out of a tenth-story window from this hotel. His death happened nearly a week after he had been secretly dosed with LSD, suffered a psychotic break, resigned from his post, and began therapy with an MKULTRA-associated physician Harold Abramson. Suspicions around his death have never been cleared, but Olson's family received an out-of-court settlement for his death and an apology from former President Gerald Ford.

Left: A photo of Donald Ewen Cameron, who ran the Montreal Experiments for MKULTRA in Canada. Cameron used electroshock therapy, sensory deprivation, induced comas, and many other inhumane techniques to find a way to systematically force information out of interrogation subjects. Many have likened his experiments to torture. Many of his patients, who were to be treated for depression or schizophrenia, regressed while under his care, often suffering from incontinence and amnesia after undergoing tests. Many patients forgot how to talk and began to believe their interrogators were their parents.

Vietnam's Declassified Bombshell

On June 13, 2011, the U.S. government declassified 7,000 pages of a study entitled "Report of the Office of the Secretary of Defense Vietnam Task Force." The wordily titled study's release was not a random choice; it was the fortieth anniversary of its controversial leak to the press in 1971. At that time, the report was better known by its much catchier nickname: the Pentagon Papers.

As the war dragged on, American support for U.S. government actions in the region shrunk. People lost faith in the government's assurances that the war was winnable, and the anti-war mood grew into protests, demonstrations, and even riots. In the midst of this turmoil, a reporter for the *New York Times* by the name of Neil Sheehan was tipped off to the existence of a highly classified report. The report detailed U.S. political and military involvement in Vietnam from 1945 to 1967. Sensing a big story, Sheehan contacted Daniel Ellsberg, an ex-U.S. Marine Corp officer and former strategic analyst for the Department of Defense.

At the beginning of the war, Ellsberg had been a supporter of U.S. involvement in the region and helped to compile the report at the end of the study in 1967. A few years later, however, Ellsberg, like so many other Americans, had come to believe the war was a lost cause. And what's more, he believed that the American people had a right to know what was contained in the lengthy, secretive report.

So, in June of 1971, with doubts about the government's actions weighing on his mind, Ellsberg—who, by this time, was working as a senior research associate at MIT's Center for International Studies—decided to turn over portions of the report to Sheehan. And on June 13, the *New York Times* published the first of a series of front page articles about the report, which revealed that several presidential administrations had misled the public on U.S. involvement in Vietnam. The report even revealed that the John F. Kennedy administration had an active part of the overthrow and assassination of South Vietnamese President Ngo Dinh Diem in 1963. The publication of these bombshells set off a media frenzy, and the report was quickly dubbed the Pentagon Papers.

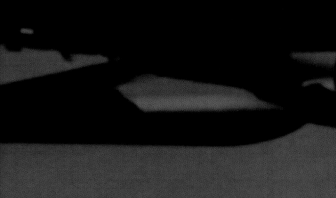

Robert McNamara, Secretary of Defense for both President Kennedy and Johnson, pointing to a map of Vietnam in 1965. For the large part, McNamara was responsible for the build up of American troops in South Vietnam due to his fears that a communist Vietnam would spread communism's influence in the region.

By 1971, the United States had been entrenched in the Vietnam War for sixteen long years. The conflict waged between pro-communist North Vietnam, backed by the Soviet Union and China, and anti-communist South Vietnam, which was backed by the United States, South Korea, and Australia.

Needless to say, the Nixon administration was not happy to see government secrets splashed across the front page of the *New York Times*. After only three articles had been published, the U.S. Department of Justice got a temporary restraining order against the *Times*, citing a threat to national security. This did not sit well with the newspaper, which fought back in the case of New York Times Co. v. United States. While the *Times* was tied up in court, the *Washington Post* picked up the slack and began publishing their own articles featuring the Pentagon Papers. Once again, the government attempted to silence the publication; however, this time they were not successful. As the *Post* continued to publish articles and the case made its way to the Supreme Court, ten other newspapers across the country got their hands on the report and started publishing their own articles. The Pentagon Papers had taken on a life of their own.

Ultimately, on June 30, 1971, the Supreme Court ruled 6-3 in favor of the media, and all news organizations across the country were free to publish whatever parts of the report they chose. The Nixon administration indicted Ellsberg on criminal charges of conspiracy, espionage, and stealing government property, but those charges were later dropped when it was discovered that a secret team had broken into Ellsberg's psychiatrist's office to find information about him.

President Kennedy with Secretary of Defense McNamara. During Kennedy's presidency, with McNamara's recommendation, the number of American troops in Vietnam increased from 900 to 16,000.

Top: A 1957 photo of President Eisenhower and South Vietnam's president Ngo Dihm Diem, who rose to power in the region with the backing of the U.S. government. Diem was later assassinated during an American backed coup in 1963.

Bottom: U.S. aircrafts over Vietnam during Operation Rolling Thunder. The Pentagon Papers revealed that although American officials lacked confidence in the effectiveness of the American campaign in Vietnam, they continued to futilely increase military presence in the region.

Chapter 2

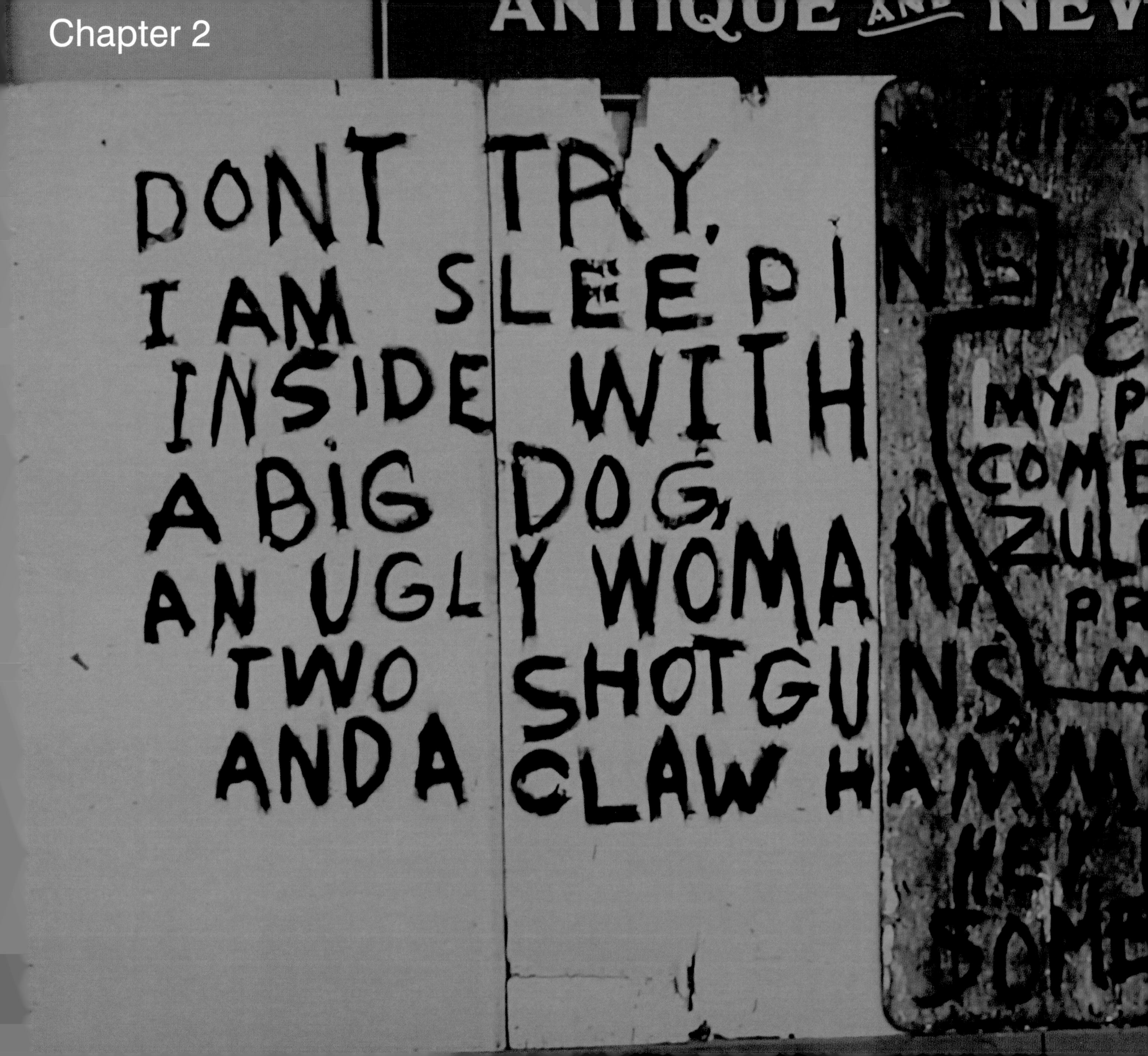
ANTIQUE AND
DONT TRY.
I AM SLEEPIN
INSIDE WITH
A BIG DOG,
AN UGLY WOMAN,
TWO SHOTGUNS
AND A CLAW HAMM

Disasters, Tragedies & Accidents

San Francisco: April 18, 1906

The Great San Francisco Earthquake–a 7.8 magnitude tremor–brought down structures across the Bay Area. In San Francisco, buildings crumbled, water mains broke, and streetcar tracks twisted into metal waves. But the majority of the 3,000 deaths and $524 million in property damage came from the massive post-tremor fire, which spread rapidly across the city in the absence of water to quell the flames. People as far away as southern Oregon and western Nevada felt the shaking, which lasted nearly a minute.

The statue of Louis Agassiz fell off Stanford University's Zoology building during the quake.

Fires burning after the San Francisco earthquake that hit the city April 18, 1906.

Another photo taken after the quake looking at the fire from Sacramento Street.

Central California:
October 18, 1989

The Loma Prieta quake–which struck the San Francisco area as game three of the 1989 World Series was just about to begin in Candlestick Park–killed 63 people and caused property damage of approximately $6 billion. At 6.9 on the Richter scale, it was the strongest shake in the Bay Area since 1906. Al Michaels, an ABC announcer in the ballpark for the game, was later nominated for an Emmy for his live earthquake reports.

Above: The collapsed upper deck of the San Fransisco-Oakland Bay Bridge.

Left: Five people were killed under this building's collapsing facade on San Francisco's Sixth Street between Bluxome and Townsend Avenues.

Top: A photo of a car being crushed by a building's third floor after the Loma-Prieta quake.

Bottom: The Cypress Street Viaduct of Interstate 880 collapsed during the quake in Oakland, California.

Alaska:
March 28, 1964

The most powerful tremor in U.S. history—lasting three minutes and measuring 9.2 on the Richter scale—struck Prince William Sound in Alaska. Only 15 people died in the quake itself, but the resulting tsunami, which reached more than 200 feet high at Valdez Inlet, killed 110 more people and caused $311 million in property damage. The city of Anchorage was hit particularly hard, with 30 downtown blocks suffering heavy damage.

A photo of a man inspecting a plank of wood that was driven through a tire from the force of the quake's resulting tsunami.

The largest landslide caused by the earthquake hit the area around the Knik Arm waterway in Anchorage. Any semblance of solid ground is completely absent in this photo.

Florida Keys & Corpus Christi, Texas: September 1919

This was the only Atlantic hurricane to form in 1919, but it was a monster! With winds reaching 140 miles per hour, the category 4 storm originally made landfall in Key West, Florida, but continued over the warm waters of the Gulf of Mexico and struck again in Corpus Christi—now downgraded to category 3, but with a 12-foot storm surge. The storm cost more than $22 million in damages and killed between 600 and 900 people—many of them passengers on ten ships lost in the Gulf of Mexico. Coincidentally, a boy named Bob Simpson survived the Corpus Christi leg of the storm, sparking his interest in hurricanes and eventually leading him to codevelop the Saffir-Simpson scale used to measure hurricane strength.

Front page of the *Seattle Star* tells of the devastation after the hurricane.

Okeechobee Hurricane: September 1928

Reaching category 5 strength when it slammed Puerto Rico, the storm then hit Palm Beach, Florida, with 150-mile-per-hour winds and little warning. Coastal residents were prepared, but 40 miles inland at Lake Okeechobee, the massive rainfall that accompanied the storm crumbled a six-foot-tall mud dike around the lake. The storm cost $100 million in damages and killed more than 1,800 people, although some estimates list the death toll as high as 4,000.

Cleaning the debris from Olive Street, West Palm Beach after the hurricane.

Damage in West Palm Beach after the hurricane.

Great Labor Day Storm: September 1935

I n little more than 24 hours, this storm went from a category 1 to a category 5, where it remained when it struck the Florida Keys, making it the first hurricane of such intensity to strike the United States. With wind speeds reaching 200 miles per hour and a 15-foot storm surge, this cataclysmic hurricane caused $6 million in damages. Of the more than 420 people killed in the storm, about 260 of them were World War I veterans who were in the region building bridges as part of President Roosevelt's New Deal. The flimsy camps that housed the veterans were no match for this wicked storm, and the train sent to rescue them was blown off the tracks.

The Florida East Coast Railway Overseas Railroad was derailed during the hurricane near Islamorada, Florida.

A group of men cleaning up and collecting the bodies of those who died during the hurricane.

A mass burial of the veterans who died during the hurricane.

New England Hurricane: September 1938

Normally, hurricanes thrive on the warm, tropical waters along the southeastern coast of the United States. But this storm had other plans, striking the northeastern United States instead. With winds gusting at more than 100 miles per hour, the eye of this hurricane struck Long Island, New York, but winds and massive rainfall wreaked havoc in Massachusetts, Connecticut, and Rhode Island, and caused damage in Montreal as well. Dubbed the "Long Island Express," the storm killed 700 people, injured 700 more, and caused $306 million in damages. It also brought a 12- to 16-foot storm surge that destroyed more than 8,000 homes and 6,000 boats.

Flooding on Beaver Street in Keene, New Hampshire.

A photo of the flooding at Buzzards Bay railroad station in Massachusetts.

Flooding in Hartford, Connecticut's Bushnell Park after the hurricane.

Hurricane Camille:
August 1969

With wind gusts exceeding 200 miles per hour and a 20-foot storm surge, Camille was the second category 5 hurricane to hit the United States. The massive storm struck along the mouth of the Mississippi River and flattened nearly everything along Mississippi's coastline. After pounding the Gulf Coast, Camille moved inland and caused heavy flooding and landslides in Virginia. In total, Camille caused more than $1.4 billion in damages and 259 deaths.

Damaged eastbound lanes of Interstate 90 after Camille hit.

Damage in Biloxi, Mississippi.

Ships beached in Gulfport, Mississippi.

Hurricane Andrew:
August 1992

The third category 5 storm to hit U.S. shores and the first severe hurricane to hit southern Florida in 27 years, Hurricane Andrew brought along 145 mile per hour winds (with gusts up to 170 miles per hour) and a 17-foot storm surge. The day after Andrew ravaged southern Florida, it moved across to Louisiana, weakening to category 3 status but still packing 120 mile per hour winds. Andrew left 44 dead and caused $26.5 billion in damage, mostly in Florida.

Hurricane Andrew pictured from above at peak intensity just east of the Bahamas on August 23, 1992.

A piece of wood driven through the trunk of a royal palm tree.

Homestead Air Force Base was heavily damaged during Hurricane Andrew.

Hurricane Ivan: September 2004

I van was the fourth major hurricane of the busy 2004 season. At one time a category 5 storm, by the time Ivan struck at Gulf Shores, Alabama, it had weakened to category 3 status with wind speeds reaching 130 miles per hour. But Ivan was the storm that wouldn't die! After devastating much of the Florida panhandle, Ivan dumped water across the southeastern United States, then drifted over the Atlantic Ocean. Once back over the water, Ivan built enough energy to loop around to the south, move across the Florida peninsula, and pick up steam over the Gulf of Mexico—again! Here, the remnants of the storm intensified and made landfall as a tropical storm along the coast of Louisiana. When Ivan finally dissipated over Texas, the storm had left 121 people dead and had caused more than $19 billion in damages.

A photo of Hurricane Ivan taken from the International Space Station.

The winds at Pensacola Beach were so severe that cars were picked up and thrown into the ocean.

Pensacola Beach, Florida, was covered in sand due to the highs winds and the storm surge.

Hurricane Katrina: August 2005

The year 2005 was another busy year for hurricanes, and Katrina, the fifth hurricane of the season, was one that will go down in history. Katrina made landfall near Buras-Triumph, Louisiana, with winds reaching 125 miles per hour before devastating the entire Gulf Coast of Mississippi. But all eyes were on New Orleans, situated below sea level and surrounded by rivers and lakes. So when Katrina made landfall slightly to the east, people in "The Big Easy" breathed a sigh of relief since it appeared that Mississippi had borne the major brunt of the storm. But that changed a few hours later when the massive rainfall and storm surge caused Lake Ponchartrain to flood. When the city's levee system was breached in several places, eighty percent of New Orleans was left under water. The rest of the nation watched via television as residents stayed on rooftops in the scorching heat for days awaiting rescue. The U.S. government was severely criticized for its delayed reaction in sending aid. Katrina's wrath took more than 1,800 lives and hundreds are still missing. With more than $81 billion in damages, Katrina was the most expensive natural disaster in U.S. history.

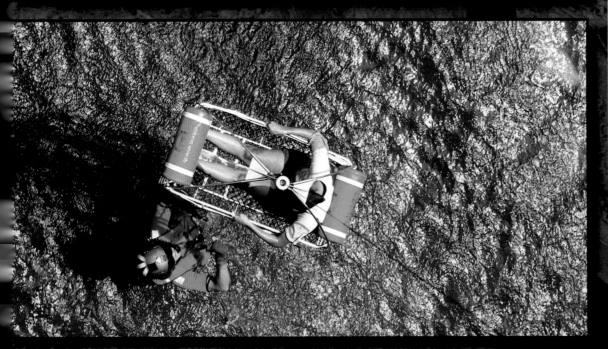

The Interstate 10 and Interstate 610 interchange flooded in northwes New Orleans.

he U.S. Coast Guard airlifting a pregnant woman to safety during a search and rescue mission on August 30, 2005.

The flood waters reached so high in New Orleans' Ninth Ward that many residents fled to their roofs to stay above the rising water.

New York City's Violent Past

T he city presents itself like Rocky: It can take a punch and keep swinging. Given that New York remains standing after the following haymakers, the image is deserved.

Great Fire of New York →
This conflagration that consumed the west side of southern Manhattan started on September 21, 1776, probably in a waterfront tavern, during the colonial defense of the city against the British. Some 400 to 500 buildings were destroyed.

A depiction of the fire. The British are depicted in their redcoats attacking American revolutionaries.

←The Peach Tree War
In September 1655, New Amsterdam governor Peter Stuyvesant marshaled troops to attack New Sweden (in modern Delaware). Furious Native Americans promptly raided New Amsterdam, Hoboken, and Staten Island. The burning and looting that followed left about 100 colonists dead, and 100 or more were taken hostage.

Peter Stuyvesant seen here with his peg leg in *The Fall of New Amsterdam*.

←Chatham Square Fire
On May 19, 1811, high winds gusting to gale force turned a factory blaze into a pyre for 100 buildings. A general short-age of water available to firefighters was an early wake-up call about the city's future needs.

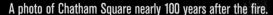
A photo of Chatham Square nearly 100 years after the fire.

↑Long Island Hurricane
The first major hurricane in the city's history hit at Jamaica Bay on September 3, 1821. The 13-foot storm surge flooded Battery Park and lower Manhattan as far as Canal Street. While damaging, the flood caused few deaths.

The storm caused a record surge on the southern tip of Mahattan Island where Battery Park, pictured here, is located. The flooding has only been surpassed by the flooding caused by Hurricane Sandy, 191 years later.

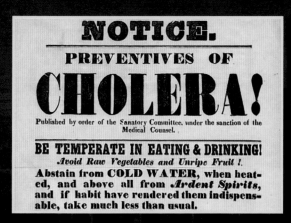

NOTICE.

PREVENTIVES OF

CHOLERA!

Published by order of the Sanatory Committee, under the sanction of the Medical Counsel.

BE TEMPERATE IN EATING & DRINKING!
Avoid Raw Vegetables and Unripe Fruit !.
Abstain from **COLD WATER**, when heated, and above all from *Ardent Spirits*, and if habit have rendered them indispensable, take much less than usual.

◂Cholera Epidemics

In 1832, 1848-49, and 1866, cholera outbreaks killed thousands at a time. Indelicately put, the ailment killed with diarrhea that led to irreversible fluid loss. Early treatments included opium suppositories and tobacco enemas—neither of which is recommended for home treatment today!

Handbill from the New York City Board of Health, 1832.

Great Financial District Fire➤

On December 16-17, 1835, city firefighters discovered that water is very hard to pump when the air temperature is 17 degrees Fahrenheit. This largely unchecked blaze incinerated 500 buildings around Wall Street, including most of the few remaining Dutch-era structures.

The fire blazed so bright that night that it was supposedly visible from Philadelphia, some 80 miles away.

⬥Brooklyn Theatre Fire

On December 5, 1876, theatergoers who had gathered to see a popular French melodrama, *The Two Orphans*, were sent into panic when fire broke out at the Brooklyn Theatre. Many of the 278 dead were children in the cheap seats, where fire-escape provisions were inadequate.

Front page of *Frank Leslie's Illustrated Newspaper* showing people trying to identify the relics of the victims.

◂*Westfield II* Ferry Explosion

The boiler of this Staten Island steamer blew up at Manhattan dockside on July 30, 1871, killing 125 and injuring about 140.

A wood engraving illustrating the retrieval of the accident's victims.

Great Blizzard of 1888

New York tried to absorb snowdrifts of 20 feet or more and winds in excess of 45 mph, when a late-winter storm slammed the Atlantic coast from Maryland to Maine. Two hundred of the storm's 400 deaths occurred in New York City.

A photo of the Brooklyn Bridge during the storm.

Heat Wave of 1896➤

During the long span of August 5-13, sustained temperatures above 90 degrees Fahrenheit scorched people in tenements, sometimes lethally. In the end, 420 or more people died, mostly in the overcrowded squalor of the Lower East Side.

A street market in the streets of New York before the turn of the twentieth century.

➤Triangle Shirtwaist Fire

On March 25, 1911, a carelessly tossed match or cigarette started a fast-spreading fire inside Max Blanck and Isaac Harris's shirtwaist (blouse) sweatshop, which occupied the eighth, ninth, and tenth floors of Manhattan's Asch Building. Grossly inadequate fire exit provisions, plus locked inner doors, spelled disaster. Most of the 146 dead were immigrant women, mainly Jewish. Those that did not burn to death died of smoke inhalation or from injuries sustained when they leapt from windows.

A photo of several victims' bodies being placed in coffins on the sidewalk.

➤*General Slocum* Disaster

Until 9/11, June 15, 1904, was New York's deadliest day. During a church picnic aboard a chartered steamboat in the East River, more than 1,000 people, most of them German-American women and children, died when the triple-deck, wooden ship caught fire.

Firefighters trying to extinguish the fire as *General Slocum* lists into the East River.

Wall Street Bombing

Was it a car bomb that exploded in the financial district on September 16, 1920? No, it was a horse-drawn wagon bomb carrying 100 pounds of dynamite and hundreds of pounds of iron that went up in front of 23 Wall Street. The massive explosion killed 38 people and wounded more than 300. No perpetrator was ever found, but authorities unofficially blamed two popular bogeymen of the day: anarchists and Communists.

A victim being taken away on a gurney after the bombing.

1943 Harlem Riots

When a black G.I. who tried to prevent a white police officer from manhandling a black woman was shot, simmering racial tensions ignited. It was August 1, 1943, and throughout the night and into the following day, rioters destroyed property across Harlem. Six African Americans died, and hundreds of people (including 40 cops) were injured. At least 500 people were arrested.

Holland Tunnel Fire

New York City officials have good reasons for banning highly explosive carbon disulfide from being driven through the Holland Tunnel. On Friday, May 13, 1949, a 55-gallon drum of the solvent fell off a truck and caught fire. The blaze spread quickly, engulfing many of the 125 vehicles that were in the tunnel at the time, and ravaging the structure's ceiling and walls. An FDNY battalion chief was felled by smoke and died four months later. Sixty-six people were injured.

The Holland Tunnel is still in use today with nearly 90,000 cars using it per day in 2016. Traffic in the tunnel, especially commercial traffic, has declined since restrictions were put in place following the 9/11 attacks.

TWA Flight 266/United Flight 826

Snow, rain, and fog, plus pilot error, precipitated the December 16, 1960, midair collision of a TWA Constellation and a United DC-8 some 5,200 feet above the city. United Flight 826 had been badly off course. The DC-8 fell onto Brooklyn's Park Slope neighborhood, killing six people on the ground. The Constellation disintegrated on impact and crashed at Miller Field on Staten Island. All 128 people on the two planes perished, although an 11-year-old boy aboard the DC-8 survived long enough to describe the crash to authorities.

A DC-8 aircraft that is similar to the one involved in the December 16th incident.

Chapter 3

Unexplained
Phenomena

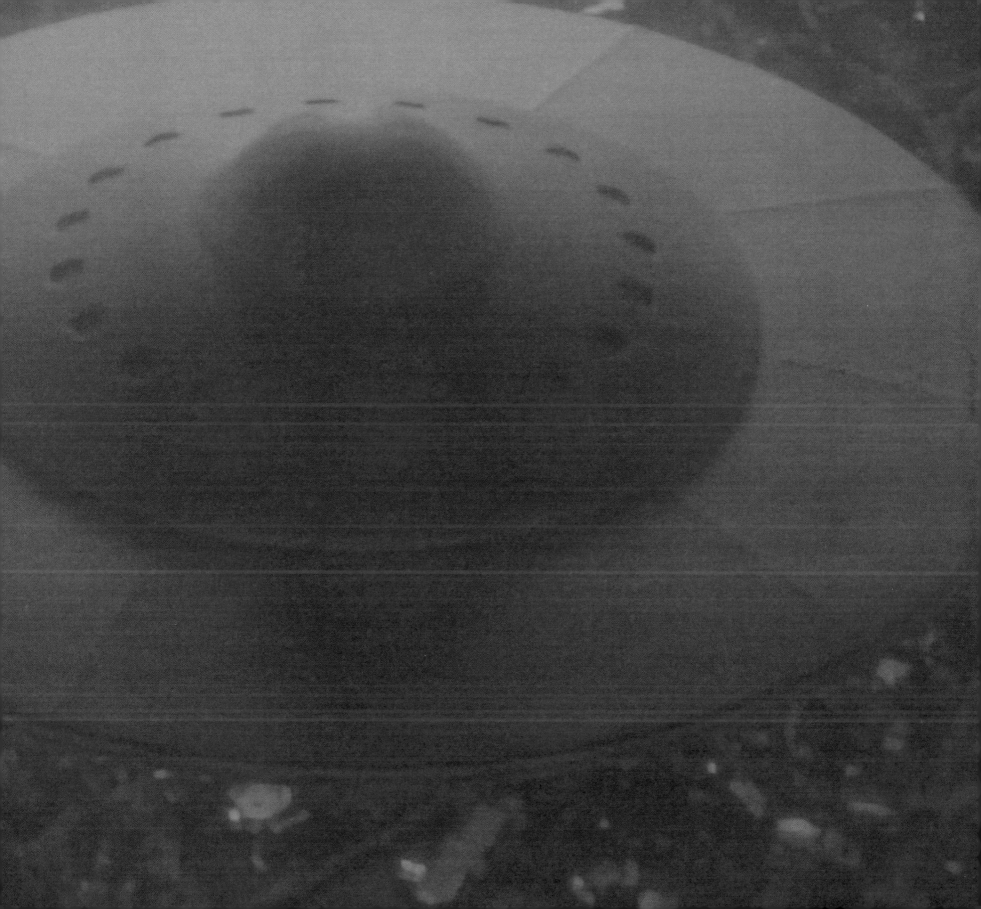

Former CIA Director Calls for UFO Transparency

Dedicated to his country, Vice-Admiral Roscoe H. Hillenkoetter climbed the ranks of the Navy during both World Wars and became the first director of the Central Intelligence Agency in 1947. But despite his access to the intelligence community, even he questioned whether or not the U.S. government and the military generals of the Air Force were transparent in what they knew about the subject of UFOs. Maybe Hillenkoetter felt a bit of interdepartmental suspicion toward the Air Force, or maybe he knew more than what was admitted to the public.

After his time directing the CIA and his retirement from the Navy, Hillenkoetter joined the board of the National Investigations Committee of Aerial Phenomenon (NICAP) with the intention of persuading the government to disclose the information it held on UFOs to the public. In the June 1, 1960, edition of the *Worcester Evening Gazette*, Hillenkoeter claims "The unknown objects are operating under intelligent control. It is imperative to learn where the UFOs come from and what their purpose is."

Hillenkoetter referred to objects he had seen during his service in the intelligence community, and he later states that what he saw was in no ways technologically possible for Russia or the U.S. to develop. He called for a congressional investigation into the U.S. Air Force because he believed they were not telling the truth about UFOs. It remains unclear as to what Hillenkoetter had seen during his life, but whatever it was, he believed it was something that should not be kept from the public.

Roscoe H. Hillenkoeter was an exemplary citizen, naval officer, and patriot by any standard. But he, like many others, have questioned the truthfulness of the American government regarding UFOs.

Throughout the World War II, Roscoe H. Hilenkoetter continued to climb the ranks of the naval intelligence community to then be promoted by President Truman to Director of the Central Intelligence Agency in 1947.

Hillenkoeter was trained at the United States Naval Academy in Annapolis, Maryland, in 1919, and then went to serve in the Atlantic Fleet during World War I. As World War II broke out in Europe, Hillenkoeter served as an Allied coordinator of underground militias in Vichy France. He was injured in the attack on Pearl Harbor serving as Executive Officer of the USS *West Virginia* (pictured above).

The John Lennon song "Nobody Told Me" touches on his experience with a UFO. In 1974, the former Beatle reported seeing a UFO outside his apartment in New York City. As he and a friend watched, the UFO drifted away, changing its shape with each rotation. Lennon took photos of the craft, but when he attempted to develop the film, it turned out blank. Lennon's friend called the police, who had received two other calls on the incident, and the *New York Daily News*, which had received five calls reporting a UFO on the East Side that night. *The New York Times* allegedly hung up on him.

John Lennon might not be the most credible source for a UFO report due to his association with psychedelic drugs. Lennon was also monitored for some time by the FBI because of his anti-war views and links to radical politics.

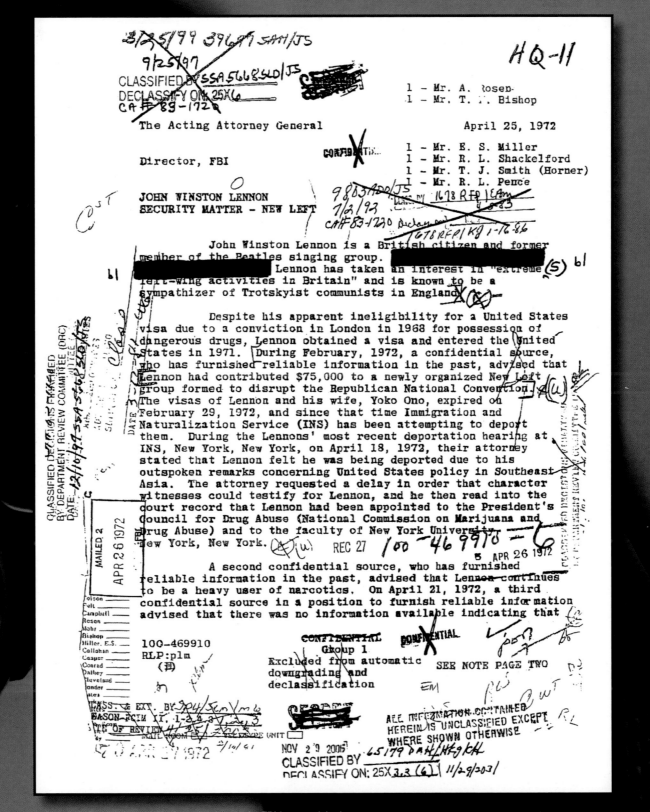

A declassified and censored file from the dossier the FBI kept on John Lennon.

An Astronaut With
Unpopular Views

Astronaut Gordon Cooper participated in a United Nations panel discussion on UFOs in New York in 1985. In the discussion, Cooper said, "I believe that these extraterrestrial vehicles and their crews are visiting this planet from other planets, which obviously are a little more technically advanced than we are here on Earth. I feel that we need to have a top-level, coordinated program to scientifically collect and analyze data from all over the Earth concerning any type of encounter, and to determine how best to interface with these visitors in a friendly fashion."

Gordon Cooper (foreground) and Charles Conrad Jr. in the *Gemini-5* craft moments before the hatch was closed. Along with Project Gemini, Cooper also worked on Project Mercury and Project Apollo.

Project Mercury

In 1959, the National Aeronautics and Space Administration (NASA) selected 110 pilots to be tested for the new Mercury space program. The following finalists became the Mercury Seven: Scott Carpenter, Gordon Cooper, John Glenn, Virgil "Gus" Grissom, Walter Schirra, Alan Shepard, and Donald "Deke" Slayton.

The Mercury missions were NASA's first efforts at sending humans into space and then recovering them. The first two missions lasted only about 15 minutes and demonstrated that the method worked (mainly, that nothing blew up and you could get the astronaut back alive). On the third, U.S. Marine John Glenn earned fame by becoming the first American to orbit Earth. On the sixth and last, Gordon Cooper stayed up for 34 hours and made 22 orbits.

The orbital and suborbital flights revealed important information about how humans handle space travel. The astronauts were guinea pigs, returning home to every medical test, poke, and prod one can imagine. The project's success represented an important Cold War boost for U.S. prestige and national morale during the tense Cuban Missile Crisis years, and its lessons proved essential for the 1969–72 *Apollo* lunar landings. The Mercury Seven, who shared a bond like no other, remained close for the rest of their lives.

Ronald Reagan

ormer actor and U.S. president Ronald Reagan witnessed UFOs on two occasions. Once during his term as California governor (1967–1975), Reagan and his wife Nancy arrived late to a party hosted by actor William Holden. Guests including Steve Allen and Lucille Ball reported that the couple excitedly described how they had just witnessed a UFO while driving along the Pacific Coast Highway. They had stopped to watch the event, which made them late to the party.

Reagan also confessed to a *Wall Street Journal* reporter that in 1974, when the gubernatorial jet was preparing to land in Bakersfield, California, he noticed a strange bright light in the sky. The pilot followed the light for a short time before it suddenly shot up vertically at a high rate of speed and disappeared from sight. Reagan stopped short of labeling the light a UFO, of course.

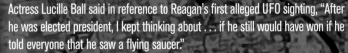

Actress Lucille Ball said in reference to Reagan's first alleged UFO sighting, "After he was elected president, I kept thinking about . . . if he still would have won if he told everyone that he saw a flying saucer."

Reagan's Cold War Concerns

Ronald Reagan is considered the first president to talk about the possibility of an alien invasion. He believed that if such a situation occurred, all the nations of the world should unite to fight off the attackers. Reagan even discussed this scenario with General Secretary Mikhail Gorbachev during their first summit meeting in Geneva in 1985.

Here we see a photo of President Reagan talking with General Secretary Gorbachev at their 1985 summit in Geneva.

Jimmy Carter

During Jimmy Carter's presidential election campaign of 1976, he told reporters that he once saw what could have been a UFO in 1969, before he was governor of Georgia. "It was the darndest thing I've ever seen," he said of the incident. He claimed that the object that he and a group of others had watched for ten minutes was as bright as the moon.

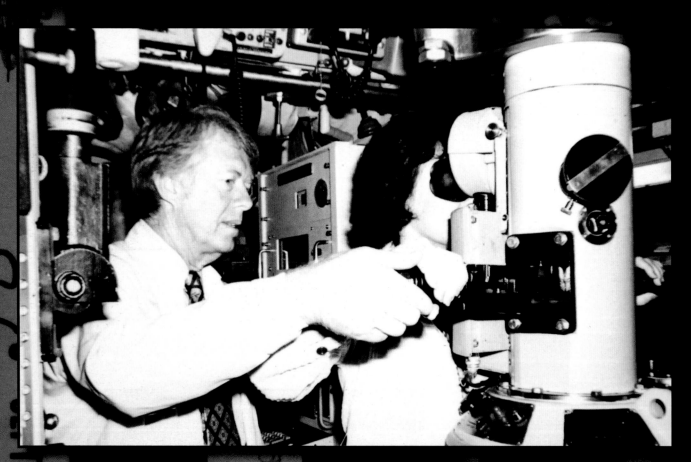

Carter was often referred to as "the UFO president" after being elected because he filed a report on the matter. Here we see him aboard the USS *Los Angeles* with First Lady Rosalynn Carter.

STATEMENT

This Voyager spacecraft was constructed by the United States of America. We are a community of 240 million human beings among the more than 4 billion who inhabit the planet Earth. We human beings are still divided into nation states, but these states are rapidly becoming a single global civilization.

We cast this message into the cosmos. It is likely to survive a billion years into our future, when our civilization is profoundly altered and the surface of the Earth may be vastly changed. Of the 200 billion stars in the Milky Way galaxy, some -- perhaps many -- may have inhabited planets and spacefaring civilizations. If one such civilization intercepts Voyager and can understand these recorded contents, here is our message:

> This is a present from a small distant world, a token of our sounds, our science, our images, our music, our thoughts and our feelings. We are attempting to survive our time so we may live into yours. We hope someday, having solved the problems we face, to join a community of galactic civilizations. This record represents our hope and our determination, and our good will in a vast and awesome universe.

Jimmy Carter

President of the United States
of America

THE WHITE HOUSE,
June 16, 1977

NASA

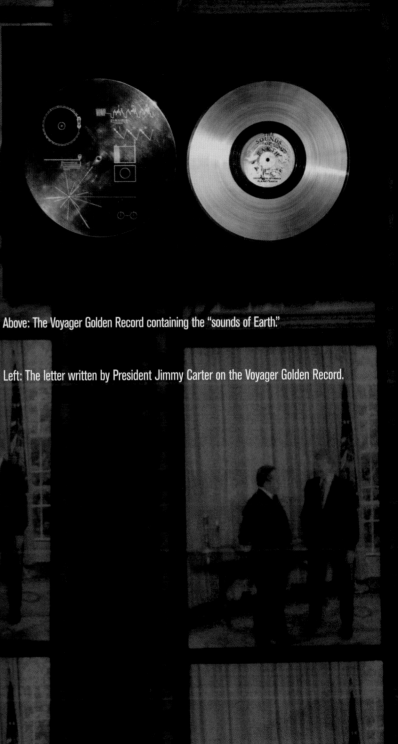

Above: The Voyager Golden Record containing the "sounds of Earth."

Left: The letter written by President Jimmy Carter on the Voyager Golden Record.

Renowned Reports of UFOs

Unidentified flying objects, foo fighters, ghost rockets—whatever you call them, strange and unclassified objects in the sky remain one of the world's truly mysterious phenomena. Here are some of the most famous UFO sightings.

The Battle of Los Angeles

On February 25, 1942, just weeks after Japan's attack on Pearl Harbor and America's entry into World War II, late-night air-raid sirens sounded a blackout order throughout Los Angeles County in California. A silvery object (or objects) was spotted in the sky, prompting an all-out assault from ground troops. For a solid hour, antiaircraft fire bombarded the unidentified craft with some 1,400 shells, as numerous high-powered searchlights followed its slow movement across the sky. Several witnesses reported direct hits on the invader, though it was never downed. After the "all clear" was sounded, the object vanished, and it has never been identified.

Page B of the *Los Angeles Times* on February 26, 1942.

The Marfa Lights

The town of Marfa, located far out in western Texas, is home to what many believe is the best concentration of "ghost lights" in the nation. Almost nightly, witnesses along Highway 67 can peer across the flatland north of the Chinati Mountains and spot glowing orbs of varying color and size, bobbing and floating among the brush. It's an event that's reportedly been witnessed since the 1880s. Though several scientists have conducted studies, no one has been able to determine their origin. Nevertheless, local officials have capitalized on the phenomenon and constructed an official roadside viewing area.

Due to how common the sightings of the Marfa Lights are, many scientists suggest that the lights are caused by atmospheric reflections of headlights, although the lights have been observed since before automobiles were invented.

The Washington Flap

In two separate incidents just days apart in 1952, numerous objects were detected high above Washington, D.C., moving erratically at speeds as fast as 7,000 miles per hour. At one point, separate military radar stations detected the same objects simultaneously. Several eyewitnesses viewed the objects from the ground and from air control towers, and three pilots spotted them at close range, saying they looked like the lit end of a cigarette or like falling stars without tails. The official Air Force explanation was "temperature inversion," and the sightings were labeled "unexplained."

The lights were first detected by air-traffic controller Edward Nugent at the Ronald Reagan International Airport located on the Potomac River. Nugent spotted seven objects on his radar flying erratic flight patterns 15 miles southwest of Washington, D.C. Fighter jets were scrambled to the area, but the objects disappeared until the jets ran low on fuel and returned to the skies. The objects were last detected by radar four hours after they were initially spotted.

The Hill Abduction, aka the Zeta Reticuli Incident

By the 1960s, a number of people had reportedly seen UFOs but hadn't actually encountered aliens personally. But on September 19, 1961, Barney and Betty Hill found themselves being chased by a spacecraft along Route 3 in New Hampshire. The object eventually descended upon their vehicle, whereupon Barney witnessed several humanoid creatures through the craft's windows. The couple tried to escape, but their car began shaking violently, and they were forced off the road. Suffering lapses in memory from that moment on, the Hills later recalled being taken aboard the ship, examined, and questioned by figures with very large eyes. The incident was known only to locals and the UFO community until the 1966 publication of *The Interrupted Journey* by John Fuller.

Barney and Betty Hill with their dog Desley

Fire in the Sky

After completing a job along Arizona's Mogollon Rim on November 5, 1979, Travis Walton and six fellow loggers spotted a large spacecraft hovering near the dark forest road leading home. Walton approached the craft on foot and was knocked to the ground by a beam of light. Then he and the craft disappeared. Five days later, Walton mysteriously reappeared just outside of town. He said that during his time aboard the spacecraft, he had struggled to escape from the short, large-headed creatures that performed experiments on his body. Neither Walton nor any of his coworkers has strayed from the facts of their stories in nearly 40 years.

A view from the Mogollon Rim looking over the Tonto National Forest.

The *Apollo* 11 Transmission

When American astronauts made that great leap onto the surface of the moon on July 20, 1969, they apparently weren't alone. Although the incident has been repeatedly denied, believers point to a transmission from the lunar surface that had been censored by NASA but was reportedly picked up by private ham-radio operators: "These babies are huge, sir! Enormous!... You wouldn't believe it. I'm telling you there are other spacecraft out there, lined up on the far side of the crater edge. They're on the moon watching us!"

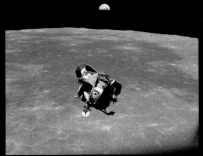

Left: A photo of Buzz Aldrin on the moon, taken by mission commander Neil Armstrong. What they saw and felt that day can never be known.

Right: The Lunar Module *Eagle* ascending back toward Command Module *Columbia*.

Japanese Airlines Flight 1628

On November 17, 1986, as Japan Airlines flight 1628 passed over Alaska, military radar detected an object on its tail. When the blip caught up with the cargo jet, the pilot reported seeing three large craft shaped like shelled walnuts, one of which was twice the size of an aircraft carrier. The objects matched the airplane's speed and tracked it for nearly an hour. At one point, the two smaller craft came so close that the pilot said he could feel their heat. The incident prompted an official FAA investigation and made worldwide headlines.

The sighting lasted for nearly 50 minutes and ended in the vicinity of Mount Denali, North America's tallest mountain.

The Phoenix Lights

In March 1997, hundreds, if not thousands, of witnesses throughout Phoenix, Arizona, and the surrounding area caught sight of what was to become the most controversial UFO sighting in decades. For at least two hours, Arizona residents watched an array of lights move across the sky, and many reportedly saw a dark, triangular object between them. The lights, which varied in color, were even caught on videotape. Nearby military personnel tried to reproduce the event by dropping flares from the sky, but most witnesses weren't satisfied with what was deemed a diversion from the truth.

Skies, phone lines light up Ariz.

By Scott Troyanos

Unidentified: For 106 minutes on March 13, people saw something like this V-shaped object flying over Arizona. UFOs? The only thing certain is that it still haunts them. **4A.**

A clipping from *USA Today* featuring an illustration of the object by witness Tim Ley.

The United States government's response to the Phoenix Lights incident claims that the lights were military flares deployed by A-10 Warthogs during a test at the Barry Goldwater Air Force Range southwest of Phoenix.

Roswell

Undoubtedly the most famous UFO-related location, Roswell immediately brings to mind flying-saucer debris, men in black, secret military programs, alien autopsies, weather balloons, and government cover-ups. The incident that started it all occurred during the first week of July 1947, just before Roswell Army Air Field spokespersons claimed they had recovered parts of a wrecked "flying disc" from a nearby ranch. The report was quickly corrected to involve a weather balloon instead, which many insist was part of a cover-up. In later years, people claiming to have been involved in the recovery effort began to reveal insider information, insisting that not only was the wreckage of extraterrestrial origin, but that autopsies had been performed on alien bodies recovered from the site. Ever since, the name of this small New Mexico town has been synonymous with ufology, making Roswell a popular stop for anyone interested in all things alien.

Left: An aerial photo of the Walker Air Force Base, the base where the supposedly recovered flying disk was kept, near Roswell, New Mexico.

Right: A photo of a National Oceanic and Atmospheric Administration weather balloon, the type of balloon used in the government's explanation.

The Lost Viking Settlement

According to ancient Norse sagas that were written in the thirteenth century, Leif Eriksson was the first Viking to set foot in North America. After wintering at the place we now call Newfoundland in the year 1000, Leif went home. In 1004, his brother Thorvald led the next expedition, composed of thirty men, and met the natives for the first time. The Vikings attacked and killed eight of the nine native men they encountered. A greater force retaliated, and Thorvald was killed. His men then returned home.

Six years later, a larger expedition of Viking men, women, and livestock set up shop in North America. They lasted two years, according to the sagas. The Vikings traded with the locals initially, but they soon started fighting with them and were driven off. There may have been one further attempt at a Newfoundland settlement by Leif and Thorvald's sister, Freydis.

In 1960, Norse ruins of the appropriate age were found in L'Anse aux Meadows, Newfoundland, by Norwegian couple Helge and Anne Stine Ingstad. The Vikings had been there, all right. Excavations over the next seven years uncovered large houses and ironworks where nails and rivets were made, as well as woodworking areas. Also found were spindlewhorls, weights that were used when spinning thread; this implies that women were present, which suggests the settlement was more than a vacation camp.

The ruins don't reveal why the Vikings left, but they do confirm what the old sagas claimed: The Vikings were in North America. The sagas say that the settlers fought with the local *Skraelings*, a Norse word meaning "natives," until the *Skraelings* came at them in large enough numbers to force the Vikings out. This sounds plausible, given the reputation of the Vikings—they'd been raiding Europe for centuries—and the Eriksson family's history of violence. Would you want neighbors like them?

A woodcut frontispiece of Erik the Red from a 1688 Icelandic publication. Erik the Red, the father of Leif, founded a Greenland colony because he'd been thrown out of Iceland for murder, and Erik's father had been expelled from Norway for the same reason.

Above: Leif Eriksson discovering America in Christian Krohg's 1893 painting.

Left: *The Landing of the Vikings* by Arthur C. Michael, depicting Leif and his crew landing on the shores of Newfoundland, Canada.

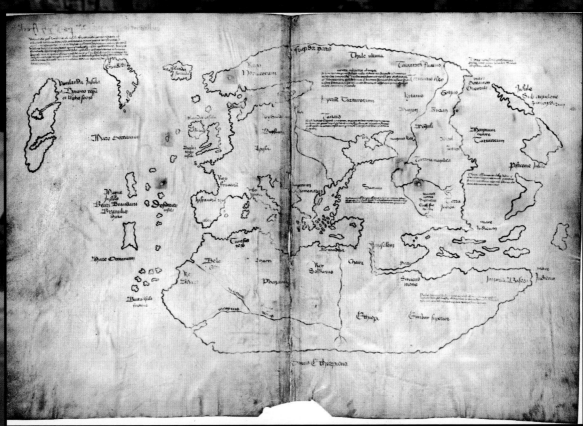

A map alleged to be made before Columbus discovered the Americas depicting Vinland on the far left.

Dorothy Arnold

After spending most of December 12, 1910, shopping in Manhattan, American socialite Dorothy Arnold told a friend she was planning to walk home through Central Park. She never made it. Fearing their daughter had eloped with her one-time boyfriend George Griscom, Jr., the Arnolds immediately hired the Pinkerton Detective Agency, although they did not report her missing to police until almost a month later. Once the press heard the news, theories spread like wildfire, most of them pointing the finger at Griscom. Some believed he had murdered Arnold, but others thought she had died as the result of a botched abortion. Still others felt her family had banished her to Switzerland and then used her disappearance as a cover-up. No evidence was ever found to formally charge Griscom, and Arnold's disappearance remains unsolved.

POLICE DEPARTMENT
CITY OF NEW YORK.

LOOK FOR--MISSING

Miss Dorothy H. C. Arnold
Of No. 108 East 79th Street
New York City

The Knickerbocker Trust Co., located at Fifth Avenue and 27th Street, the intersection where Arnold was last reported seen.

KNICKERBOCKER TRUST CO., 234 FIFTH AVENUE, CORNER OF 27TH STREET.

Many theories try to explain Dorothy Arnold's disappearance, but her disappearance remains unsolved. One theory claims that Dorothy acquired amnesia after she slipped and injured her head. Another rumor claims that she might have died during an attempt to abort a pregnancy that she had been hiding from her family.

Central Park, 1901.

Disappearance From Alcatraz

Officially, records show that there was never a successful escape from Alcatraz Prison while it was in operation. Of course, those records leave out the part that three men might have made it, but they disappeared in the process.

On June 11, 1962, after spending two years planning their escape, inmates Frank Morris and brothers Clarence and John Anglin placed homemade dummies in their bunks, crawled through hand-dug tunnels, and made their way to the prison roof. Then they apparently climbed down, hopped aboard homemade rafts, and made their way out into San Francisco Bay.

The next day, one of the largest manhunts in history began. Pieces of a raft and a life preserver were found floating in the bay, as well as a bag containing personal items from the escapees, but that was all. The official report stated that in all likelihood, the men drowned. However, a 2003 episode of *Mythbusters* determined that the men may have survived.

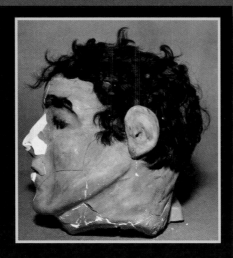

Dummy head found in Frank Morris' cell. The broken nose resulted when the head rolled off the bed and struck the floor after a guard reached through the bars and pushed it.

Headshot of Frank Morris on January 20, 1960.

Above: One of the prison cells in which the escape was made. Beneath the sink you can see the widened vent opening.

Top Left: Headshot of John Anglin on October 24, 1960.

Bottom Left: Headshot of Clarence Anglin on January 10, 1961.

D. B. Cooper

On the evening of November 24, 1971, a man calling himself Dan Cooper (later known as D. B. Cooper) hijacked an airplane, and demanded $200,000 and four parachutes, which he received when the plane landed in Seattle. Cooper allowed the plane's passengers to disembark but then ordered the pilot to fly to Mexico. Once the plane had gained enough altitude, somewhere over the Cascade Mountains near Woodland, Washington, Cooper jumped from the plane to never be seen again. Despite a massive manhunt, no trace of him has ever been found. In 1980, an eight-year-old boy found nearly $6,000 in rotting $20 bills lying along the banks of the Columbia River. A check of their serial numbers found that they were part of the ransom money given to Cooper, but what became of the rest of the money, and Cooper, is a mystery to this day.

A BULLETIN FROM THE F.B.I

FOLLOWING IS AN ARTIST CONCEPTION OF THE HIJACKER WHO EXTORTED $200,000 FROM NORTHWEST AIRLINES ON NOVEMBER 24, 1971.

THIS MAN IS DESCRIBED AS FOLLOWS:

RACE	WHITE
SEX	MALE
AGE	MID 40'S
HEIGHT	5' 10'' TO 6'
WEIGHT	170 TO 180 POUNDS
BUILD	AVERAGE TO WELL BUILT
COMPLEXION	OLIVE, LATIN APPERANCE, MEDIUM SMOOTH
HAIR	DARK BROWN OR BLACK, NORMAL STYLE, PARTED ON LEFT, COMBED BACK; SIDEBURNS, LOW EAR LEVEL
EYES	POSSIBLY BROWN. DURING LATTER PART OF FLIGHT PUT ON DARK, WRAP-AROUND SUNGLASSES WITH DRAK RIMS
VOICE	LOW, SPOKE INTELLIGENTLY; NO PARTICULAR ACCENT, POSSIBLY FROM MIDWEST SECTION OF U.S.
CHARACTERISTICS	HEAVY SMOKER OF RALEIGH FILTER TIP CIGARETTES
WEARING APPAREL	BLACK SUIT; WHITE SHIRT; NARROW BLACK TIE; BLACK DRESS SUIT; BLACK RAIN-TYPE OVERCOAT OR DARK TOP COAT; DARK BRIEFCASE OR ATTACHE CASE; CARRIED PAPER BAG 4" X 12" X 14"; BROWN SHOES.

IF YOU HAVE ANY INFORMATION WHICH MIGHT LEAD TO THE IDENTITY OF THIS INDIVIDUAL, PLEASE CONTACT THE NEAREST FBI OFFICE WHICH WOULD BE FOUND IN THE FRONT OF YOUR TELEPHONE DIRECTORY.

The FBI bulletin with information concerning D.B. Cooper's hijacking.

Ongoing Investigation

A photo of a portion of the cash found along the Columbia River in 1980. Thousands of leads have been investigated over the years. The case remains the only unsolved hijacking in U.S. history. Late in 2007, the FBI's Seattle field office kick-started the investigation, providing pictures on its website of some key evidence, including the money and Cooper's black clip-on tie.

Agent Larry Carr continues to work the case. He, like agents who came before him, believes he knows what happened to Cooper, who jumped into a wind of two hundred miles per hour in total darkness on a cold and rainy night. "Diving into the wilderness without a plan, without the right equipment, in such terrible conditions," Carr says, "he probably never even got his chute open."

Jimmy Hoffa

On the afternoon of July 30, 1975, Jimmy Hoffa, former president of the International Brotherhood of Teamsters, stepped onto the parking lot of the Manchus Red Fox Restaurant near Detroit and into history. Scheduled to meet with known mobsters from New Jersey and New York, Hoffa vanished and was never seen or heard from again. Since that day, wild theories involving mob hits and political assassinations have run rampant. But despite hundreds of anonymous tips, confessions from mob hitmen, and even the wife of a former mobster accusing her husband of the hit, it is still unknown what happened to Hoffa or where he's buried, and the case officially remains open. As recently as May 2006, FBI agents were still following leads and digging up yards in Michigan trying to find out what happened to Hoffa.

James "Jimmy" R. Hoffa (left) with his son James P. Hoffa at a testimonial dinner in 1964, the year criminal charges were put against him for bribery and fraud.

Hoffa's last known location.

FD-36 (Rev. 8-29-85)

FBI

TRANSMIT VIA:
☒ Teletype
☐ Facsimile
☐ AIRTEL

PRECEDENCE:
☒ Immediate
☐ Priority
☐ Routine

CLASSIFICATION:
☐ TOP SECRET
☐ SECRET
☐ CONFIDENTIAL
☒ UNCLAS E F T O
☐ UNCLAS

Date 7/24/92

FM FBI DETROIT (183A-1155) (C-8) (P)

TO DIRECTOR FBI/IMMEDIATE/ (183-6421) (9-60052)

BT

UNCLAS E F T O

CITE: //3220//

PASS: HQ SSA ████████████ DC/DB SECTION 2 (INFO); HQ

SSA ████████ MEDIA SECTION (INFO); BROOKLYN - QUEENS

MRA, A/SAC NORTH (ACTION).

SUBJECT: HOFFEX; OO: DETROIT.

RE TELCALS ON JULY 24, 1992, BETWEEN SAS ████████ AND

████████ WITH HQ AND ASAC A.T. RIGGIO, DETROIT AND ASAC

DON NORTH, BROOKLYN QUEEN MRA. BE ADVISED A 70 YEAR OLD EX-

CON DETAILS HIS VERSION OF HOFFA'S KILLING IN AN INTERVIEW

THAT AIRS ON "A CURRENT AFFAIR" TONIGHT, FRIDAY, JULY 24,

1992, AT 7:30 P.M., ON NATIONAL TELEVISION. THE UNSUB WHO

SPEAKS ON CAMERA, BUT IS NOT IDENTIFIED, STATES HE WAS ONE OF

TMC/gls

(1)   183A-1155-833

Approved: _____ Original filename: GISOO2 SO.206!

Time Received: _____ Telprep filename: _____

MRI/JULIAN DATE: 1122/206   ISN: 006

FOX DATE & TIME OF ACCEPTANCE: 7/23/92   1718

One of the many declassified FBI documents pertaining to Hoffa's disappearance.

SECRETS OF AMERICAN HISTORY   77

The Mysteries of the Bermuda Triangle

F ew geographical locations on Earth have been discussed and debated more than the three-sided chunk of ocean between the Atlantic coast of Florida and the regions of San Juan, Puerto Rico, and Bermuda known as the Bermuda Triangle.

Over the centuries, hundreds of ships and dozens of airplanes have mysteriously disappeared while floating in or flying through the region commonly called the Bermuda Triangle. Myth mongers propose that alien forces are responsible for these dissipations. Because little or no wreckage from the vanished vessels has ever been recovered, paranormal pirating has also been cited as the culprit. Other theorists suggest that leftover technology from the lost continent of Atlantis—mainly an underwater rock formation known as the Bimini Road (situated just off the island of Bimini in the Bahamas)—exerts a supernatural power that grabs unsuspecting intruders and drags them to the depths.

Although the theory of the Triangle had been mentioned in publications as early as 1950, it wasn't until the '60s that the region was anointed with its three-sided appellation. Columnist Vincent Gaddis wrote an article in the February 1964 edition of *Argosy* magazine that discussed the various mysterious disappearances that had occurred over the years and designated the area where myth and mystery mixed as the "Deadly Bermuda Triangle." The use of the adjective deadly perpetrated the possibility that UFOs, alien anarchists, supernatural beings, and metaphysical monsters reigned over the region. The mystery of Flight 19, which involved the disappearance of five planes in 1945, was first noted in newspaper articles that appeared in 1950, but its fame was secured when the flight and its fate were fictitiously featured in Steven Spielberg's 1977 alien opus, *Close Encounters of the Third Kind*. In Hollywood's view, the pilots and their planes were plucked from the sky by friendly aliens and later returned safely to terra firma by their abductors.

Possible explanations for this region's strange history of disappearances include the Gulf Stream's uncertain current, the high volume of sea and air traffic in the region, and even methane hydrates (gas bubbles) that produce "mud volcanoes" capable of sucking a ship into the depths.

The daughter of former vice president Aaron Burr, Theodosia Burr, was swept up by the sea in the Bermuda Triangle in 1812 when the sea schooner *Patriot*, a commercial vessel, never arrived in New York after leaving South Carolina.

The Bermuda Triangle is an infamous stretch of the Atlantic Ocean bordered by Florida, Bermuda, and Puerto Rico where strange disappearances have occurred throughout history. The Coast Guard doesn't recognize the Triangle or the supernatural explanations for the mysterious disappearances.

In 1975, historian, pilot, and researcher Lawrence David Kusche published one of the first definitive studies that dismissed many of the Triangle theories. In his book *The Bermuda Triangle Mystery—Solved*, he concluded that the Triangle was a "manufactured mystery," the result of bad research and reporting and, occasionally, deliberately falsified facts. Before weighing anchor on Kusche's conclusions, however, consider that one of his next major publications was a tome about exotic popcorn recipes.

The Coast Guard receives almost 20 distress calls every day from amateur sailors attempting to navigate the slippery sides of the Triangle. Modern-day piracy—usually among those involved in drug smuggling—has been mentioned as a probable cause for odd occurrences, as have unusual magnetic anomalies that alter compass readings.

Some pragmatists have insisted that a combination of natural forces—a double whammy of waves and rain that create the perfect storm—is most likely the cause for these maritime misfortunes. Other possible "answers" to the mysteries include rogue waves (such as the one that capsized the *Ocean Ranger* oil rig off the coast of Newfoundland in 1982), hurricanes, underwater earthquakes, and human error.

Flight 19

On the afternoon of December 5, 1945, five Avenger torpedo bombers left the Naval Air Station at Fort Lauderdale, Florida, with Lt. Charles Taylor in command of a crew of 13 student pilots. About 90 minutes into the flight, Taylor radioed the base to say that his compasses weren't working, but he figured he was somewhere over the Florida Keys. The lieutenant who received the signal told Taylor to fly north toward Miami, as long as he was sure he was actually over the Keys. Although he was an experienced pilot, Taylor got horribly turned around, and the more he tried to get out of the Keys, the further out to sea he and his crew traveled. As night fell, radio signals worsened, until, finally, there was nothing at all from Flight 19. A U.S. Navy investigation reported that Taylor's confusion caused the disaster, but his mother convinced them to change the official report to read that the planes went down for "causes unknown." The planes have never been recovered.

A photo of five U.S. Navy Avengers, similar to those lost in 1945.

The *Spray*

Joshua Slocum, the first man to sail solo around the world, never should have been lost at sea, but it appears that's exactly what happened. In 1909, the *Spray* left the East Coast of the United States for Venezuela via the Caribbean Sea. Slocum was never heard from or seen again and was declared dead in 1924. The ship was solid, and Slocum was a pro, so nobody knows what happened. Perhaps he was felled by a larger ship or maybe he was taken down by pirates. No one knows for sure that Slocum disappeared within the Triangle's waters, but Bermuda buffs claim Slocum's story as part of the area's mysterious and supernatural legacy.

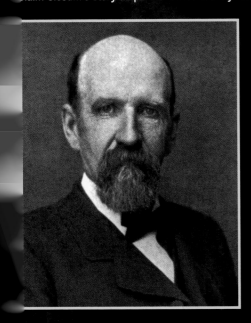

Left: Joshua Slocum, the first man to sail around the world by himself, was lost in the Bermuda Triangle in 1909.

Right: A photo of the *Spray*, the gaff-rigged sloop sailboat Slocum used to sail solo around the world in 1895.

USS *Cyclops*

As World War I heated up, America went to battle. In 1918, the *Cyclops*, commanded by Lt. G. W. Worley, was sent to Brazil to refuel Allied ships. With 309 people onboard, the ship left Rio de Janeiro in February and reached Barbados in March. After that, the *Cyclops* was never seen or heard from again. The navy says in its official statement, "The disappearance of this ship has been one of the most baffling mysteries in the annals of the navy, all attempts to locate her having proved unsuccessful. There were no enemy submarines in the western Atlantic at that time, and in December 1918, every effort was made to obtain from German sources information regarding the disappearance of the vessel."

The USS *Cyclops* descended to its watery repository without a whisper in March 1918 with 309 people aboard. Myth suggests supernatural subterfuge, but the reality is that violent storms or enemy action were the likely culprits.

Star Tiger

The *Star Tiger*, commanded by Capt. B. W. McMillan, was flying from England to Bermuda in early 1948. On January 30, McMillan said he expected to arrive in Bermuda at 5:00 a.m., but neither he nor any of the 31 people onboard the *Star Tiger* were ever heard from again. When the Civil Air Ministry launched an investigation, they learned that the *S.S. Troubadour* had reported seeing a low-flying aircraft halfway between Bermuda and the entrance to Delaware Bay. If that aircraft was the *Star Tiger*, it was drastically off course. According to the Civil Air Ministry, the fate of the *Star Tiger* remains unknown.

An Avro Tudor aircraft similar to the *Star Tiger*, which was lost over the Bermuda Triangle on January 30, 1948.

Flight 201

This Cessna left for Fort Lauderdale on March 31, 1984, en route for Bimini Island in the Bahamas, but it never made it. Not quite midway to its destination, the plane slowed its airspeed significantly, but no distress signals came from the plane. Suddenly, the plane dropped from the air into the water, completely vanishing from the radar. A woman on Bimini Island swore she saw a plane plunge into the sea about a mile offshore, but no wreckage has ever been found.

A Cessna 402B, similar to the one flown on Flight 201.

Chapter 4

Conspiracy Theories

Conspiracies Surrounding JFK's Assassination

Conspiracy theories are a favorite American pastime, right up there with alien abductions and Elvis sightings. Perhaps no conspiracy theories are more popular than the ones involving that afternoon in Dallas—November 22, 1963—when the United States lost a president. John F. Kennedy's life and death have reached out to encompass everyone from Marilyn Monroe to Fidel Castro, Sam Giancana to J. Edgar Hoover.

The Single-Shooter Theory:

This is the one the Warren Commission settled on–that Lee Harvey Oswald (and only Lee Harvey Oswald), firing his Mannlicher-Carcano rifle from the window of the Texas Book Depository, killed the president in Dealey Plaza. But this is the official finding, and where's the excitement in that?

A photo of Lee Harvey Oswald holding his Mannlicher-Carcano rifle, which cost just $30, and two Marxist newspapers. This photograph, along with two others like it, became critical pieces of evidence because they connected the rifle that was left at the depository with Oswald.

A photo of the Texas Book Depository taken four months after the assassination where witness Howard Brennan sat during the incident. "A" indicates where Brennan claims to have seen Oswald shooting from the building, while "B" shows where he saw several people watching the motorcade.

Two-Shooter Theory:

A second shooter on the nearby grassy knoll fired at the same time as Oswald. His bullets hit Texas Governor John Connally and struck President Kennedy from the front. This theory arose after U.S. Marine sharpshooters at Quantico tried to duplicate the single-shooter theory but found it was impossible for all the shots to have come from the Book Depository.

John Connally was critically wounded during the incident, suffering from three broken ribs, a punctured lung, a shattered wrist, and a bullet lodged into his thigh. The Warren Commission, which investigated the assassination, concluded that a single bullet passed through President Kennedy's throat and then through Connally's torso, arm, and leg. Connally often doubted the Warren Commission's analysis and questioned whether or not one bullet could have caused so much damage. If Connally's and Kennedy's wounds were inflicted by two bullets, and if you consider the short amount of time between their injuries, many believe that two shooters are necessary to explain the incident.

The CIA Theory:

After Kennedy forced Allen Dulles to resign as head of the CIA following the Bay of Pigs fiasco, the CIA, resenting Kennedy's interference, took its revenge on the president. They'd had plenty of practice helping plotters take out Patrice Lumumba of the Congo, Rafael Trujillo of the Dominican Republic, and President Ngo Dinh Diem of Vietnam.

A photo of the Three Tramps, who were suspected of possibly being a part of the assassination plot. On the day of the assassination, several photos of these men were taken as they were escorted by police near the book depository. Many conspiracy theorists believe that these men were CIA agents who also played a part in the Bay of Pigs.

The LBJ Theory:

Lyndon Johnson's mistress, Madeleine Brown, said that the vice president met with powerful Texans the night before the killing. She claimed he told her, "After tomorrow those goddamn Kennedys will never embarrass me again–that's no threat–that's a promise." Jack Ruby also implicated LBJ.

During his term as vice president under the Kennedy presidency, Lyndon Johnson continually tried to increase the responsibility, visibility, and influence of the vice presidency. Yet Kennedy refused to consider many of Johnson's requests.

Madeleine Brown and her second son Steven Mark Brown.

The Cuban Exiles Theory:

Reflecting more bitterness over the Bay of Pigs, the powerful Cuban exile community in the United States was eager to see Kennedy dead and said so. However, this probably played no part in the assassination. Also, there are other theories conjecturing the Cuban government contracted Oswald to kill Kennedy, telling him that there was an escape plan. There wasn't.

Due to Oswald's political beliefs in communism, many have linked Oswald with the Cuban government and Fidel Castro, but there is no evidence to support said claims.

The J. Edgar Hoover and the Mafia Theory:

The Mafia was said to have been blackmailing Hoover about his homosexuality for ages. The theory goes that when Attorney General Robert Kennedy began to legally pursue Jimmy Hoffa and Mafia bosses in Chicago, Tampa, and New Orleans, they sent Hoover after JFK as payback.

J. Edgar Hoover, then the director of the FBI, meeting with President Kennedy and his brother Robert Kennedy, the then U.S. Attorney General.

The Organized Crime Theory:

Chicago Mafia boss Sam Giancana, who supposedly shared the affections of Marilyn Monroe with both JFK and RFK–using Frank Sinatra as a go-between–felt betrayed when RFK went after the mob. After all, hadn't they fixed JFK's 1960 election? This theory is a tabloid favorite.

Frank Sinatra's family had many ties to the mob, and Sinatra's connection to the mob was bolstered by his working-class Italian-American image.

The Soviet Theory:

High-ranking Soviet defector Ion Pacepa said that Soviet intelligence chiefs believed that the KGB had orchestrated the Dallas killing. But they were probably just bragging.

Ion Pacepa was a general for communist Romania's secret police and worked as a CIA agent after he defected and received asylum in the U.S.

The Roscoe White Theory:

According to White's son, this Dallas police officer was part of a three-man assassination team. The junior White, however, gives no indication of the reasons behind the plot.

Many speculate that Roscoe White was the "Badge Man," who can supposedly be seen behind the fence in the center of this photo taken by Mary Moorman. They claim that White was the second gunman located here, on the Grassy Knoll, who used a sniper rifle to assassinate the president. The photo was taken fractions of a second after the shot was fired.

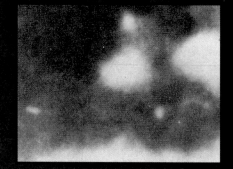

Two enlargements (one colorized) of the Moorman photograph showing the silhouette of the "Badge Man."

A professional hit man was paid $50,000 to kill Kennedy by a group of very powerful, unknown men. He was also supposed to kill Oswald. Clearly, this theory isn't thick with details.

Oswald was shot by Jack Ruby, a local nightclub owner, two days after the assassination.

Kennedy issued Executive Order 110, enabling the U.S. Treasury to print silver certificates in an attempt to drain the silver reserves. It is theorized that such a development would severely limit the economic power of the Federal Reserve. Could this have played into his assassination?

People will probably still be spinning these theories in a hundred years. But then, everyone needs a hobby.

A $1,000 Silver Certificate from 1880 featuring William Marcy, who had served as a senator and governor of New York and the Secretary of State during the Polk Administration.

The Israeli Theory:
Angry with JFK for pressuring them not to develop nuclear weapons and/or for employing ex-Nazis in the space program, the Israelis supposedly conspired in his assassination.

Many have claimed that the then prime minister of Israel, David Ben Gurion, ordered the assassination of JFK for halting Israel's nuclear weapons program.

Did Nixon Know?

Television and film star Jackie Gleason was fascinated with the paranormal and UFOs. But he had no idea that an innocent game with an influential friend would lead him face-to-face with his obsession.

An avid golfer, Gleason also kept a home close to Inverrary Golf and Country Club in Lauderhill, Florida. A famous golfing buddy lived nearby–U.S. President Richard M. Nixon, who had a compound on nearby Biscayne Bay. The Hollywood star and the controversial politician shared a love of the links, politics, and much more.

The odyssey began when Gleason and Nixon met for a golf tournament at Inverrary in February 1973. Late in the day their conversation turned to a topic close to Gleason's heart–UFOs. To the funnyman's surprise, the president revealed his own fascination with the subject, touting a large collection of books that rivaled Gleason's. They talked shop through the rest of the game, but Gleason noticed reservation in Nixon's tone, as if the aides and security within earshot kept the president from speaking his mind. He would soon learn why.

Later that evening around midnight, an unexpected guest visited the Gleason home. It was Nixon, alone. The customary secret service detail assigned to him was nowhere to be seen. Confused, Gleason asked Nixon the reason for such a late call. He replied only that he had to show Gleason something. They climbed into Nixon's private car and sped off. The drive brought them to Homestead Air Force Base in South Miami-Dade County. Nixon took them to a large, heavily guarded building. Guards parted as the pair headed inside the structure, Gleason following Nixon past labs before arriving at a series of large cases. The cases held wreckage from a downed UFO, Nixon told his friend. Seeing all of this, Gleason had his doubts and imagined himself the target of an elaborated staged hoax.

Jackie Gleason was a star of the highest order. The rotund actor kept television audiences in stitches with his portrayal of hardheaded but ultimately lovable family man Ralph Kramden in the 1955 sitcom *The Honeymooners*. He made history with his regularly aimed, but never delivered, threats to TV wife Alice, played by Audrey Meadows: "One of these days Alice, one of these days, pow, right in the kisser," and "Bang, zoom! To the moon, Alice!"

Gleason golfing with President Gerald Ford in 1975.

Leaving the wreckage, the pair entered a chamber holding six (some reports say eight) freezers topped with thick glass. Peering into the hulls, Gleason later said he saw dead bodies–but not of the human variety. The remains were small, almost childlike in stature, but withered in appearance and possessing only three or four digits per hand. They were also severely mangled, as if they had been in a devastating accident.

Returning home, Gleason was giddy. His obsession had come full circle. The enthusiasm changed in the weeks that followed, however, shifting to intense fear and worry. A patriotic American, Gleason couldn't reconcile his government's secrecy about the UFO wreckage. Traumatized, he began drinking heavily and suffered from severe insomnia.

Gleason kept details of his wild night with Nixon under wraps. Unfortunately, his soon-to-be-ex-wife didn't follow his lead. Beverly Gleason spilled the beans in *Esquire* magazine and again in an unpublished memoir on her marriage to Gleason. Supermarket tabloids ate the story up. Gleason only opened up about his night with Nixon in the last weeks of his life. Speaking to Larry Warren, a former Air Force pilot with his own UFO close encounter, a slightly boozy Gleason let his secret loose with a phrase reminiscent of his *Honeymooners* days: "We've got 'em...Aliens!"

President Nixon was a solitary man with many idiosyncrasies that were caricatured by the press. He was often misrepresented and misunderstood due to his guardedness from the fear that he would be double-crossed. When told by a journalist that many Americans felt like they didn't know him, he responded by saying, "Yeah, it's true. And it's not necessary for them to know."

Top: An aerial photo of the Homstead Air Force Base in Florida.

Bottom: Gleason was obsessed with the supernatural, and he owned a massive collection of memorabilia on the subject. It was so large and impressive that the University of Miami, Florida, put it on permanent exhibit after his death in 1987. He even had a house built in the shape of a UFO, which he christened, "The Mothership." The obsession was legendary, and it climaxed in an unimaginable way.

What About the Freemasons?

The fantastically named Most Ancient and Honorable Society of Free and Accepted Masons began like other guilds; it was a collection of artisans brought together by their common trade, in this case, stone cutting and crafting. (There are many speculations as to when the society first began. Some believe it dates back to when King Solomon's temple was built. Others believe the guild first formed in Scotland in the sixteenth century.) The Freemasons made the welfare of their members a priority. Group elders devised strict work regulations for masons, whose skills were always in demand and were sometimes taken advantage of.

The Freemason's seal, the Square and Compass, with the *G* in the center representing God, or the Grand Geometrician of the Universe.

Organized Freemasonry emerged in Great Britain in the mid-seventeenth century with the firm establishment of Grand Lodges and smaller, local Lodges. (No one overarching body governs Freemasonry as a whole, though lodges worldwide are usually linked either to England or France.) In 1730, transplanted Englishmen established the first American Lodge in Virginia, followed in 1733 by the continent's first chartered and opened Grand Lodge in Massachusetts. Boasting early American members including George Washington, Benjamin Franklin, and John Hancock, Freemasonry played a part in the growth of the young nation in ways that gradually attracted curiosity, speculation, and concern.

The source of the organization's mysterious reputation lay partly in its secrecy: Masons were prohibited from revealing secrets (some believed Masons would be violently punished if they revealed secrets, though the Masons deny such rumors). The Masonic bond also emphasized a commitment to one another. Outsiders feared the exclusivity smacked of conspiracy and compromised the motives of Masons appointed to juries or elected to public office. And nonmembers wondered about the meanings of the Freemasons' peculiar traditions (such as code words and other secretive forms of recognition between members) and symbolism (often geometric shapes or tools, such as the square and compass).

LES ASSASSINATS MAÇONNIQUES

Assassinat de William Morgar, journaliste de New-York, qui, reniant la Franc-Maçonnerie dont il avait fait partie, répara vaillamment sa faute en publiant, le premier les rituels de la secte (13 septembre 1826).

Left: For many, talk of "Freemasonry" conjures up images of intricate handshakes, strange rituals, and harsh punishment for revealing secrets about either. In actuality, the roots of the order are brotherhood and generosity. Throughout the ages, Masons have been known to fiercely protect their members and the unique features of their society.

Right: An illustration by artist Pierre Mejanel named *The Assassination of William Morgan*. William Morgan planned to publish a book that would expose the secrets of the Freemasons, but he disappeared shortly before the publication. His disappearance inspired the formation of the Anti-Mason Party which ran in opposition to Andrew Jackson's Democratic party in the 1832 presidential election.

Freemasonry in the United States suffered a serious blow in September 1826 when New York Masons abducted a former "brother" named William Morgan. Morgan was about to publish a book of Masonic secrets, but before he could, he was instead ushered north to the Canadian border and, in all likelihood, thrown into the Niagara River. His disappearance led to the arrest and conviction of three men on kidnapping charges (Morgan's body was never found)—scant penalties, locals said, for crimes that surely included murder. The affair increased widespread suspicion of the brotherhood, spawning an American Anti-Mason movement and even a new political party dedicated to keeping Freemasons out of national office.

In the decades following the Civil War, men were again drawn to brotherhood and fellowship as they searched for answers in a changing age, and Freemasonry slowly regained popularity. Today, Freemasonry remains an order devoted to its own members, charitable causes, and the betterment of society. It has a worldwide membership of at least five million. Its members are traditionally male, though certain associations now permit women. Despite the name, most members are not stonemasons. They are, however, required to have faith in a supreme being, but not necessarily the Christian god (Mohammed, Buddha, and so forth are all acceptable).

Design elements of the one-dollar bill, including the Great Seal and the "all-seeing eye," have been credited to founding fathers such as Charles Thomson and other Masons.

An etching with various symbols used by the Freemasons. The inscription at the bottom of the page reads "See, Hear, Be Silent."

Benjamin Franklin in his Freemason regalia.

Foreknowledge of Pearl Harbor

Plenty of myths have come out of World War II, but few are as unfounded as the claim that President Franklin Delano Roosevelt allowed the Japanese to attack Pearl Harbor so the United States could enter the conflict.

Conspiracy theorists frequently note that the U.S. military had successfully broken Japanese codes and thus knew in advance of the attack. This is partially true—Japanese codes had been broken, but they were diplomatic codes, not military ones. The military had received notice from other sources, including the British, that an attack was pending. What wasn't known was where the attack would take place. Almost everyone assumed it would be against the Philippines or some other Pacific territory, and no one had reason to believe that the target would be the military base at Pearl Harbor.

Another common assumption is that Roosevelt had the Pacific Fleet moved from San Diego to Pearl Harbor to lure the Japanese into attacking. However, it wasn't Roosevelt who made that decision. Rather, it was the State Department, which hoped to deter Japanese aggression with a show of naval force.

Many conspiracy theorists also like to claim that the American aircraft carriers based at Pearl Harbor had been sent on maneuvers prior to the attack as a precaution, so the attack wouldn't be as damaging as it could have been. In fact, the Japanese devastated the Pacific Fleet, sinking four U.S. battleships and severely damaging four others. In addition, three light cruisers, three destroyers, and four smaller vessels were demolished or heavily damaged, and 75 percent of the island's military air fleet was annihilated before the planes could take to the sky. The value of the aircraft carriers that survived because they were on maneuvers wouldn't be realized until months later, at the Battle of Midway.

By the time Germany began its offensive in Europe, America's relationship with Japan had deteriorated dramatically. Japan had continued to become more belligerent in 1931, and Roosevelt's support for China led Japan to sign the Tripartite Pact, aligning them with the Axis powers of Germany and Italy.

The USS *Pennsylvania* behind the wreckage of the *Downes* and *Cassin*.

A photo taken of Ford Island from a Japanese plane shortly after the attack on Pearl Harbor began. Torpedoes were deployed against ships moored on both sides of the island. In the center of the photograph, you can see the USS Virginia being hit by a torpedo on the far side of the island.

Perhaps most important is that Roosevelt didn't need a Japanese attack to bring the United States into the war. Though officially neutral at the time, the country was actively engaged in fighting the Axis by providing war materials to Great Britain and other Allied nations via the Lend-Lease Act. Furthermore, antiwar sentiment was waning dramatically as Americans grew increasingly angered by Japanese and German aggression. It was just a matter of time before the United States took off the gloves and waded into the war that was engulfing the world.

A photo of the USS *Shaw* exploding.

... we here highly resolve that these dead shall not have died in vain ...

REMEMBER DEC. 7th!

Top: A photo of the USS *Shaw* exploding from a different angle.

Bottom: A flier from the United States Office of War Information.

On July 20, 1969, millions of people worldwide watched in awe as U.S. astronauts became the first humans to step on the moon. However, a considerable number of conspiracy theorists contend that the men were just actors performing on a soundstage.

Conspiracy theorists present dozens of "examples" that supposedly prove that the moon landing never happened, and all of them are easily explained. But that hasn't kept naysayers from perpetuating the myth.

Twenty-three years after the moon landing, on February 15, 2001, Fox TV stirred the pot yet again with a program titled *Conspiracy Theory: Did We Land on the Moon?* The show trotted out the usual array of conspiracy theorists, who in turn dusted off the usual spurious "proof." And once again, NASA found itself having to answer to a skeptical but persistent few.

Top: NASA's *Apollo 11* mission launching from the Kennedy Space Station with a Saturn V rocket, a three-stage super heavy-lift launch vehicle designed by former Nazi Germany V-2 rocket engineer Wernher von Braun.

Bottom: Why was there no blast crater under the lunar module? The astronauts had slowed their descent, bringing the rocket on the lander from a maximum of 10,000 pounds of thrust to just 3,000 pounds. In addition, the lack of atmosphere on the moon spread the exhaust fairly wide, lowering the pressure and diminishing the scope of a blast crater. Here we see Neil Armstrong's shadow in the foreground with the lunar module in the background.

If the astronauts really did take photographs on the moon, why aren't the stars visible in them? The stars are there but are too faint to be seen in the photos. The reason for this has to do with the fact that the lunar surface is so brightly lit by the sun. The astronauts had to adjust their camera settings to accommodate the brightness, which then rendered the stars in the background difficult to see.

Many people theorize that the landing was faked because the United States didn't have the technology to safely send a crew to the moon. Instead, it pretended it did as a way to win the final leg of the space race against the Soviet Union. But consider the situation: Thousands of men and women worked for almost a decade (and three astronauts died) to make the success of *Apollo 11* a reality. With so many people involved, a hoax of that magnitude would be virtually impossible to contain, especially after almost four decades.

For additional proof that the moon landing really happened, consider the hundreds of pounds of moon rocks brought back by the six Apollo missions that were able to retrieve them. Moon rocks are unique and aren't easily manufactured, so if they didn't come from the moon, what is their source? Finally, there's no denying the fact that the Apollo astronauts left behind a two-foot reflecting panel equipped with dozens of tiny mirrors. Scientists are able to bounce laser pulses off the mirrors to pinpoint the moon's distance from Earth.

The myth of the faked moon landing will probably never go away. But the proof of its reality is irrefutable. In the words of astronaut Charles Duke, who walked on the moon in 1972 as part of the Apollo 16 mission: "We've been to the moon nine times. Why would we fake it nine times, if we faked it?"

Top: If there is no air on the moon, why does the flag plante by the astronauts appear to be waving? The flag appears t wave because the astronauts were rotating the pole on whic it was mounted as they tried to get it to stand upright.

Bottom: Here we see the lunar module *Eagle*'s ascent from th moon toward *Columbia*. When the lunar module took off fror the moon back into orbit, why was there no visible flame fror the rocket? The composition of the fuel used for the takeo from the surface of the moon was different in that it produce no flame.

9/11 CONSPIRACY THEORIES

September 11, 2001, will live in infamy as the nation's worst terrorist attack. Islamic extremists hijacked four commercial airliners, crashing two of the planes into the North and South towers of the World Trade Center in New York City, and a third plane into the Pentagon. A fourth airliner crashed into a field in rural Pennsylvania as passengers attempted to regain control of the aircraft from the hijackers. The 9/11 attacks killed nearly 3,000 people, injured more than 6,000, and launched an American-led war on terrorism. The attacks also provoked a wide variety of conspiracy theories. Proponents of these theories dispute some or all of the facts in the official version of the story told to the public.

A photo from the Landsat 7 satellite on the day of the attacks. You can see the smoke billowing from lower Manhattan across the Upper Bay and over New Jersey.

A firefighter looking at the remaining structure of the collapsed south tower.

106

CONTROLLED DEMOLITION THEORIES

One of the most prominent 9/11 conspiracy theories is that the collapse of both World Trade Center towers resulted from controlled demolitions using explosives planted prior to 9/11.

THEORY:

Controlled demolition theorists claim that the aircraft impacts and subsequent fires could not have weakened the buildings sufficiently to cause their collapse. They argue that jet fuel from the aircraft could not burn hot enough to melt steel. Proponents also point to clouds of dust seen blowing out of windows as evidence of explosive charges.

FACT:

The National Institute of Standards and Technology (NIST) and the magazine *Popular Mechanics*, among others, examined and rejected these theories. The NIST investigation "found no corroborating evidence for alternative hypotheses suggesting that the WTC towers were brought down by controlled demolition using explosives planted prior to Sept. 11, 2001." While the jet fuel did not melt the buildings' steel structures, it significantly weakened them. And experts identify the clouds of dust seen blowing out of the windows as air—along with pulverized concrete, paper, and other debris—being forced out of windows as floors collapsed on each other, not evidence of explosives.

Based on its comprehensive investigation, NIST concluded that the WTC towers collapsed because: "(1) the impact of the planes severed and damaged support columns, dislodged fireproofing insulation coating the steel floor trusses and steel columns, and widely dispersed jet fuel over multiple floors; and (2) the subsequent unusually large jet-fuel ignited multi-floor fires (which reached temperatures as high as 1,000 degrees Celsius) significantly weakened the floors and columns with dislodged fireproofing to the point where floors sagged and pulled inward on the perimeter columns. This led to the inward bowing of the perimeter columns and failure of the south face of WTC 1 and the east face of WTC 2, initiating the collapse of each of the towers."

A photo of a firefighter standing amongst the wreckage with a portion of United Airlines Flight 175's fuselage seen.

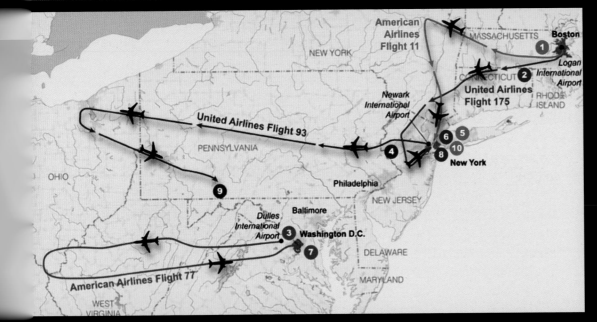

The flight paths of United Airlines Flight 175 and American Airlines Flight 11 from Boston, Massachusetts, along with American Airlines Flight 77 and United Airlines Fight 93.

THE PENTAGON ATTACK

Another prominent 9/11 conspiracy theory is that a missile, not American Airlines Flight 77, hit the Pentagon.

THEORY:

Conspiracy theorists claim that the two holes punched into the side of the Pentagon were much smaller than the wingspan of a 757.

FACT:

Investigators concluded that the main hole in the Pentagon's exterior wall, Ring E, was smaller than the plane's wingspan because one wing hit the ground and the other was sheared off on impact. The second, smaller hole in Ring C was made by the jet's landing gear.

Here are some other facts conspiracy theorists tend to dismiss or ignore:

- The remains of American Airlines Flight 77 crew and passengers were found at the Pentagon crash site, and positively identified by DNA.
- Dozens of eyewitnesses saw the plane strike the Pentagon. Some saw passengers through the plane's windows.
- Photographs and eyewitness reports show plane debris at the Pentagon crash site, as was also witnessed by survivors and rescue personnel.
- The flight's black boxes were also recovered at the site.
- Phone calls from passengers on American Airlines Flight 77 reported that it had been hijacked.
- High-ranking Al Qaeda members acknowledged that they carried out the 9/11 attacks.

The cloud of ash and debris pluming from the towers covered several surrounding blocks in Lower Manhattan.

FOREKNOWLEDGE

One of the most common 9/11 conspiracy theories is that the U.S. government had advance knowledge of the attacks and either deliberately ignored or assisted the attackers.

THEORY:

Insider trading in United Airlines and American Airlines stocks just before September 11, 2001, is evidence of advance knowledge of the plot. Allegations of insider trading in advance of September 11 generally rest on reports of unusual pre-9/11 trading activity in companies whose stock plummeted after the attacks.

FACT:

The bipartisan 9/11 Commission investigated the issue and concluded, "Some unusual trading did in fact occur, but each such trade proved to have an innocuous explanation." For example, the Commission stated in its final report, "much of the seemingly suspicious trading in American on September 10 was traced to a specific U.S.-based options trading newsletter faxed to its subscribers on Sunday, September 9, which recommended these trades."

Top Left: The wreckage after Flight 77 flew into the Pentagon.

Middle Left: A photo of the Pentagon attack from the archives of the FBI.

Bottom Left: Secretary of Defense Donald Rumsfeld inspecting the Pentagon attack site on September 11, 2001.

Middle: President George W. Bush during a joint speech to Congress on September 20, 2001, pledging "to defend freedom against terrorism."

Right: A firefighter amongst the wreckage of the World Trade Center.

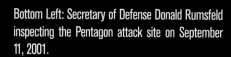

Chapter 5

Military Movements

Fort Pickens

Despite being fired upon even before Fort Sumter, Florida's Fort Pickens never fell to the Confederates.

Tradition holds that the first shots of the Civil War were fired on April 12, 1861, by Southern artillery batteries attacking Fort Sumter in the harbor of Charleston, South Carolina. Tradition is a bit off the mark, however. Hostilities actually erupted a full three months earlier, 500 miles to the southwest, and involved a fort the Union never lost to the Confederacy.

On January 8, 1861, a band of Confederate sympathizers made a midnight raid on Fort Barrancas, one of several U.S. military redoubts around Florida's Pensacola Bay that also included Fort Pickens, Fort McRee, and the Navy Yard. The band's attempt to capture Fort Barrancas was ultimately thwarted by the troops stationed there.

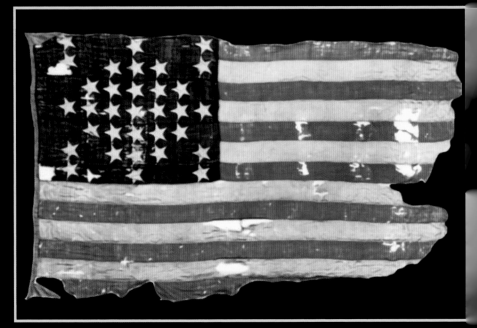

Despite the raiders' initial failure, Lieutenant Adam J. Slemmer, commander of the Union forces in the area, had apprehensions about his troop's ability to withstand a determined Confederate attack. To remedy the situation, he proceeded to spike the cannons, destroy more than ten tons of gunpowder stored at Fort McRee, and move his garrison of 80 troops just across Pensacola Pass to Fort Pickens, on the western end of Santa Rosa Island. Fort Pickens was an older, larger, somewhat dilapidated fortification that hadn't been occupied since the Mexican War. Despite the fort's shortcomings, Slemmer still believed it would be a more defensible location. He was right. Although Fort Pickens came under attack and continued to face Confederate threats, the fortress remained a Union stronghold until the conclusion of the Civil War.

A print of Fort Pickens in Pensacola Bay. Fort McRee can be seen in the background to the right.

Confederate troops firing upon Fort Pickens from Warrington, Florida's Pensacola Navy Yard.

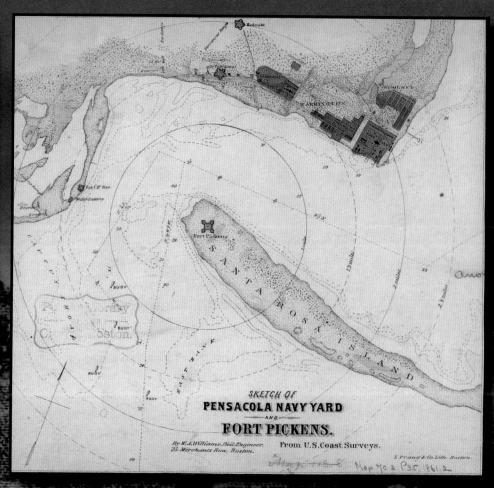

SKETCH OF
PENSACOLA NAVY YARD
AND
FORT PICKENS.

By W.J.Williams, Civil Engineer.   From U.S.Coast Surveys.
25 Merchants Row, Boston.

A map from 1861 showing Fort Pickens, located on the western edge of Santa Rosa Island, and the Pensacola Navy Yard from which Confederate troops bombarded the fort during the Civil War.

The Secrets of Skunk Works

Skunk Works—the advanced engineering branch of Lockheed and Martin—has developed some of the world's most predatory aircrafts. Founded in 1943, Skunk Works was contracted by the U.S. Air Tactical Service Command of the Army Air Force to secretly engineer a fighter jet to compete with Nazi Germany's then growing aerial force. Since then, Skunk Works has developed the U-2 and A-12 high-altitude reconnaissance aircrafts for the CIA, the SR-71 Blackbird, and the F-117 Nighthawk.

Skunk Works logo is a registered trademark of Lockheed and Martin.

Considered to be at the forefront of advanced aeronautic engineering, operations at Skunk Works are kept under close watch at the United States Air Force Plant 42 in Palmdale, California. Members of UFO communities throughout the world believe that Skunk Works has access to advanced propulsion systems and are experimenting with UFO technology. Many of these rumors are reinforced by remarks made by Skunk Works's second director, Ben Rich.

After his retirement, Rich began to surreptitiously talk about his time at Skunk Works in a correspondence with Lockheed engineer and friend John Andrews. He told Andrews, "there are two types of UFOs, the ones we build, and the ones they build...I am a believer in both categories. I feel everything is possible. Many of our man-made UFOs are Un-Funded Opportunities." Andrews also claims that Rich admitted that many of Lockheed's engineering concepts draw directly from the spacecraft that was presumably retrieved at Roswell in 1947.

A Lockheed F-35B Lightning II using Lockheed's vertical landing technology while landing on the USS *America* in 2016.

Skunk Works, the common moniker for Lockheed and Martin's Advanced Development Program, is surrounded by rumors that fall nothing short of fantastic. Here we see SR-71s being manufactured.

Ben Rich became director of Skunk Works in 1975, succeeding founding director Kelly Johnson, and was responsible for leading the development of the F-117, the world's first stealth aircraft. Here two F-117s can be seen in formation behind a B-2 Spirit bomber.

The Avrocar

Not all UFOs are alien spaceships. One top-secret program was contracted out by the U.S. military to an aircraft company in Canada.

Oh, the 1950s—a time of sock hops, drive-in movies, and the Cold War between America and the Soviet Union, when each superpower waged war against the other in the arenas of scientific technology, astronomy, and politics. It was also a time when discussion of life on other planets was rampant, fueled by the alleged crash of an alien spaceship near Roswell, New Mexico, in 1947.

Speculation abounded about the UFOs spotted nearly every week by everyone from farmers to airplane pilots. As time passed, government authorities began to wonder if the flying saucers were, in fact, part of a secret Russian program to create a new type of air force. Fearful that such a craft would upset the existing balance of power, the U.S. Air Force decided to produce its own saucer-shape ship.

In 1953, the military contacted Avro Aircraft Limited of Canada, an aircraft manufacturing company that operated in Malton, Ontario, between 1945 and 1962. Project Silverbug was initially proposed simply because the government wanted to find out if UFOs could be manufactured by humans. But before long, both the military and the scientific community were speculating about its potential. Intrigued by the idea, designers at Avro—led by British aeronautical engineer John Frost—began working on the VZ-9-AV Avrocar. The round craft would have been right at home in a scene from the classic science fiction film *The Day the Earth Stood Still*. Security for the project was so tight that it probably generated rumors that America was actually testing a captured alien spacecraft—speculation that remains alive and well even today.

An illustration depicting the Avrocar in a military setting.

By 1958, the company had produced two prototypes, which were 18 feet in diameter and 3.5 feet tall. The Avrocar was operated with a single control stick, which activated different panels around the ship. Airflow issued from a large center ring, which was controlled by the pilot to guide the craft either vertically or horizontally. The military envisioned using the craft as "flying Jeeps" that would hover close to the ground and move at a maximum speed of 40 mph.

Constructed around a large triangle, the Avrocar was shaped like a disk, with a curved upper surface. It included an enclosed 124-blade turbo-rotor at the center of the triangle, which provided lifting power through an opening in the bottom of the craft. The turbo also powered the craft's controls. Although conceived as being able to carry two passengers, in reality a single pilot could barely fit inside the cramped space.

But that, apparently, was only going to be the beginning. Avro had its own plans, which included not just commercial Avrocars, but also a family-size Avrowagon, an Avrotruck for larger loads, Avroangel to rush people to the hospital, and a military Avropelican, which, like a pelican hunting for fish, would conduct surveillance for submarines.

The prototypes impressed the U.S. Army enough to award Avro a $2 million contract. Unfortunately, the Avrocar project was canceled when an economic downturn forced the company to temporarily close and restructure. When Avro Aircraft reopened, the original team of designers had dispersed. Further efforts to revive the project were unsuccessful, and repeated testing proved that the craft was inherently unstable. It soon became apparent that whatever UFOs were spotted overhead, it was unlikely that they came from this planet. Project Silverbug was abandoned when funding ran out in March 1961, but one of the two Avrocar prototypes is housed at the U.S. Army Transportation Museum in Fort Eustis, Virginia.

Only two Avrocar prototypes were built and flight tested. Some tests showed the Avrocar was able to travel up to nearly 40 miles per hour, but the heat generated from the vehicle was so overwhelming that many of th

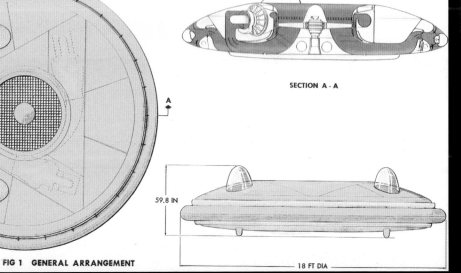

AVRO/SPG/TR254

SECRET

403 802-1

FUEL CONTROL UNIT DRAIN   FUEL PUMP SEAL DRAIN

EXHAUST DUCT
DRAIN

OVERBOARD DRAIN   COMBUSTION SYSTEM
DRAIN

VIEW ON ARROW 'A'
SHOWING ENGINE FUEL DRAINS

NOZZLE GUIDE RING   ENGINE (CONTINENTAL J69-T.9)

EXHAUST DUCT

FUEL TANK

L.P. FUEL COCK

ENGINE OIL TANK

ENGINE OIL SYSTEM VENT

ENGINE THROTTLE CONTROLS
(TELEFLEX)

ENGINE OIL TANK

FILTER

TURBOROTOR

ENGINE CONTROL
PANEL

ENGINE INSTRUMENT
PANEL

ENGINE THROTTLE
LEVERS

OIL PIPES (SUPPLY AND RETURN)

VENT PIPES (REAR BRG, ENGINE AND OIL TANK)

FUEL PIPE (TANK TO ENGINE)

FUEL DRAINS (FUEL PUMP SEAL, FUEL CONTROL
UNIT, COMBUSTION SYSTEM AND EXHAUST
DUCT DRAIN)

FIG. 14 POWERPLANT INSTALLATION

SECRET

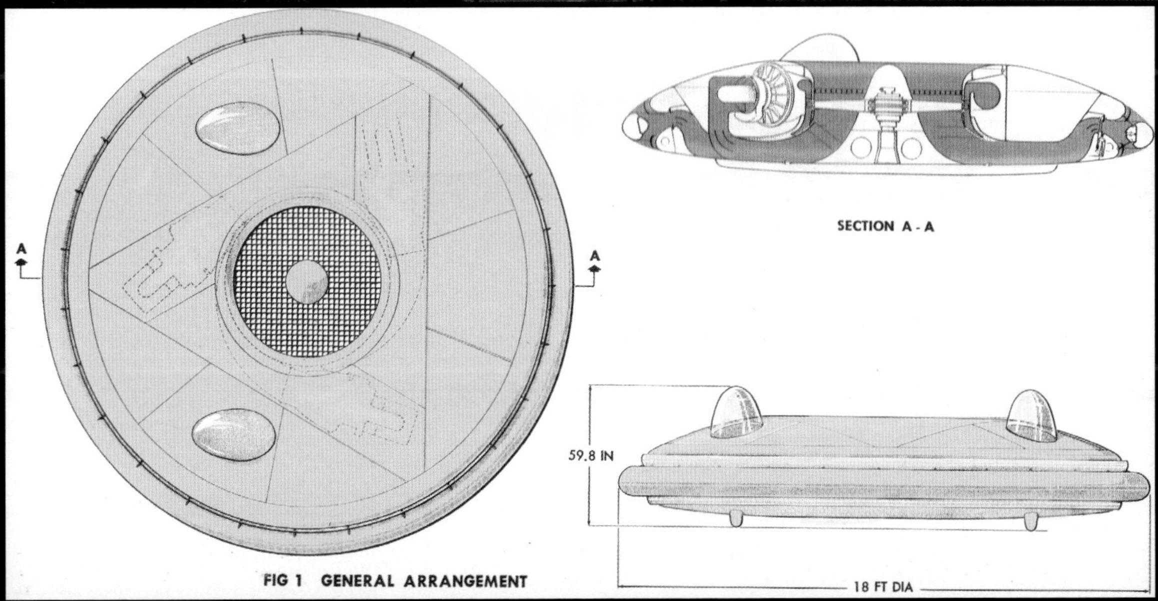

SECTION A - A

A

A

59.8 IN

18 FT DIA

FIG 1   GENERAL ARRANGEMENT

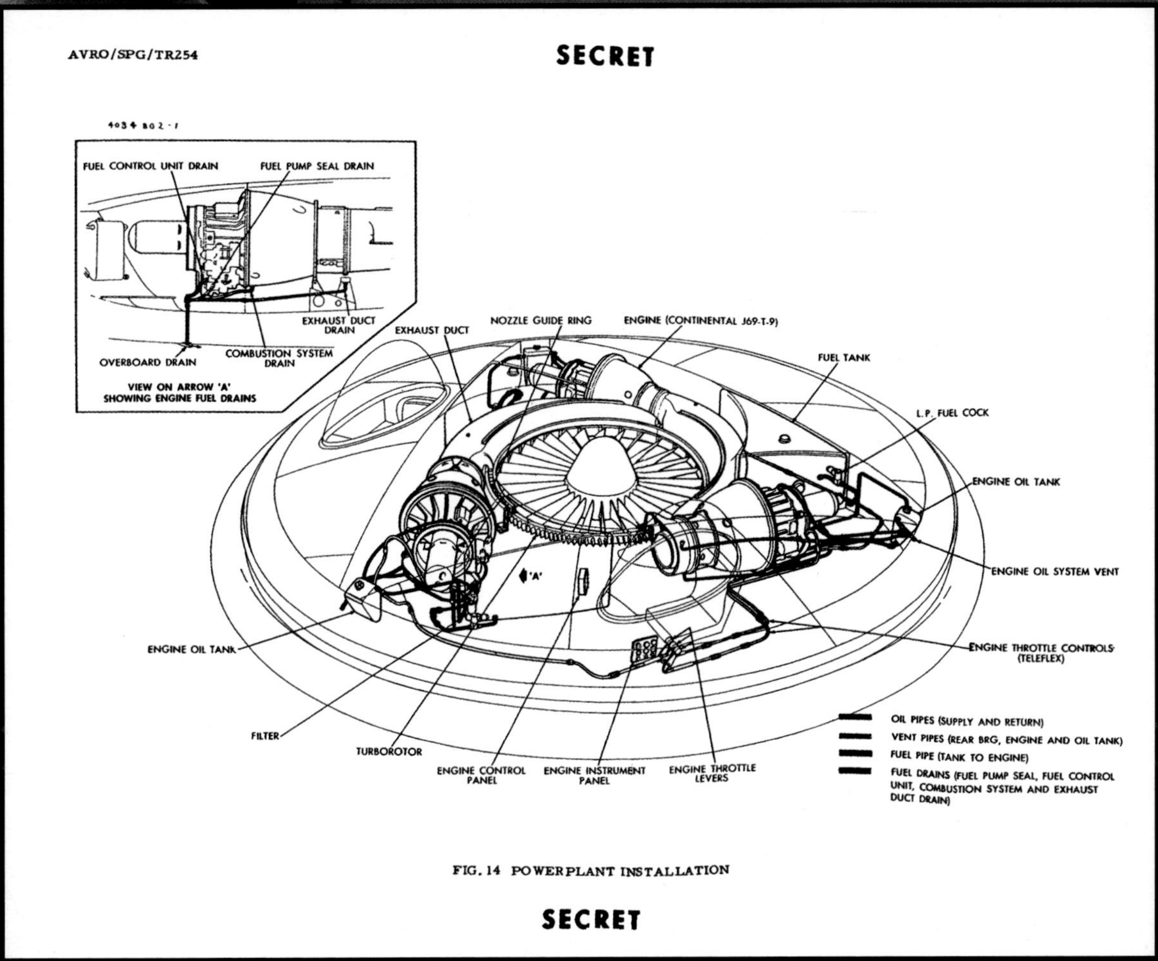

GULF OF TONKIN INCIDENT

On August 2, 1964, the destroyer USS *Maddox* was performing a signals intelligence patrol in the Gulf of Tonkin when it was pursued by three North Vietnamese Navy torpedo boats. The USS *Maddox* fired three warning shots and the North Vietnamese boats then attacked with torpedoes and machine gun fire. Three North Vietnamese torpedo boats were damaged, four North Vietnamese sailors were killed, and six more were wounded in the incident on August 2. There were no U.S. casualties and the USS *Maddox* was virtually unscathed.

On August 4, 1964, the USS *Maddox* and the destroyer Turner Joy were reportedly under attack by North Vietnamese torpedo boats. In a television address to the American public on August 4, President Lyndon B. Johnson said that the initial August 2 attack on the destroyer *Maddox* was repeated on August 4 by a number of hostile vessels attacking two U.S. destroyers with torpedoes and that he had ordered retaliatory military action in reply.

The USS *Maddox* refueling with the aircraft carrier USS *Ticonderoga* in the South China Sea in 1964. The USS *Constellation* can be seen in the background.

Days later, Congress passed the Gulf of Tonkin Resolution in response to the incident, which granted President Johnson the authority "to take all necessary steps, including the use of armed force, to assist any member or protocol state of the Southeast Asia Collective Defense Treaty requesting assistance in defense of its freedom." The resolution served as Johnson's legal justification for deploying U.S. conventional forces and the commencement of open warfare against North Vietnam.

In October 2005, the *New York Times* reported that Robert J. Hanyok, a National Security Agency historian, concluded that the NSA deliberately distorted signals intelligence (SIGINT) reports passed to policy makers regarding the August 4, 1964, incident. Hanyok argued that the SIGINT confirmed that North Vietnamese torpedo boats attacked the USS *Maddox* on August 2, 1964, although under questionable circumstances. The SIGINT also showed, according to Hanyok, that a second attack, on August 4, 1964, by North Vietnamese torpedo boats on U.S. ships, did not occur despite claims to the contrary by the Johnson administration.

A North Vietnamese gunboat under attack during Operation Piece Arrow.

Captain John J. Herrick (left) and Commander Herbert L. Ogier (right) aboard the USS *Maddox* on August 13, 1964, just days after the incident. Herrick and Ogier were in command of the *Maddox* during the incident on August 2, 1964.

The U.S. retaliated against North Vietnam, known as Operation Pierce Arrow, for the attacks by scrambling Super Hornets from the USS *Ticonderoga* and USS *Constellation* to strike torpedo boat bases in Vietnam. Here we see Super Hornets flying over the USS *Constellation*.

The Firebombing
of Dresden

Four waves of bombers hit Dresden, Germany, over three days and nights in February of 1945. The raiders dropped a mix of ordnance upon the city. The first wave used a greater proportion of higher explosives to damage buildings, exposing wood and other flammable matter. Follow-up incendiaries stoked a firestorm and high explosives hindered firefighters. The conflagration at Dresden reached temperatures of 2,700 degrees Fahrenheit, pushing a mass of superheated air above the town, causing gale-force winds to rush in, sucking people along with them.

A photo of the mosquito marker planes that deployed the target indicators on Dresden. The bombings did not have the decisive effect on German output and morale that its chief advocates hoped. Some argue, however, that the bombings did help end the war. The raids diverted major resources of the German economy into antiaircraft production and greatly weakened the Luftwaffe, which lost masses of planes and pilots in its effort to protect Germany's cities.

Survivor Lothar Metzger recalled, "Burning people ran to and fro, [there were] burnt coaches filled with civilian refugees, dead rescuers and soldiers...and fire everywhere, and all the time the hot wind of the firestorm threw people back into the burning houses they were trying to escape." Some tried taking refuge in the Old Market's historic fountain, but were broiled alive when the heat boiled the water away. Said survivor Margaret Freyer, "I saw people one after the other simply seem to let themselves drop to the ground. Today I know that these unfortunate people were the victims of lack of oxygen. They fainted and then burnt to cinders."

British after-action reports stated half the city's buildings were destroyed or severely damaged. A Dresden police report listed a toll of 647 shops, 31 hotels, 18 cinemas, 11 churches, 5 cultural buildings, 39 schools, 10 civilian hospitals, and 19 military hospitals, as well as 136 badly damaged factories and a ruined German Army headquarters. The U.S. Army Air Force reported that Dresden's "railway bridges over the Elbe River—vital to incoming and outgoing traffic—were rendered unusable for many weeks." Based on German burial records and the number of bodies found after the war, approximately 25,000 were killed in the attack.

The bombings caused firestorms that destroyed much of the city and killed approximately 25,000 people. Outdoor temperatures reached as high as 2,700 degrees Fahrenheit, making it impossible for people to escape from their doomed homes. The military efficacy of the bombings has been questioned. Dresden was poorly defended from air attack at times, and its industries were mainly on its outskirts.

Why Dresden?

During the Yalta Conference, General Aleksei Antonov, Deputy Chief of the Russian General Staff, requested that Western "air action on communications hinder the enemy from carrying out the shifting of his troops to the East...In particular, to paralyze the junctions of Berlin and Leipzig." The Western Allies pointed out to the Russians that "the structure of the Berlin-Leipzig-Dresden railway complex...required that Dresden, as well as Berlin and Leipzig, be bombed." Otherwise, the Germans could have rerouted rail traffic from the other cities through Dresden. The Allies and the Soviet Union were firmly in agreement to devastate Dresden.

U.S. Firebombs Tokyo

During World War II, U.S. leaders realized that conventional bombing missions over Japanese cities were having only a limited effect. To rectify the problem, General Curtis LeMay in 1945 implemented incendiary attacks.

LeMay recognized that the wood and paper Japanese cities were highly vulnerable to fire. Such attacks also would have a greater impact on Japanese industry, much of which was dispersed in small shops.

The incendiary of choice had been developed by Standard Oil and DuPont in 1944. Only two inches in diameter and 20 inches long, these "fire sticks" were filled with jellied gasoline or napalm and weighed about six pounds. LeMay's plan called for B-29s to scatter thousands of these devices to create unmanageable fires.

On February 23–24, the U.S. launched its first fire raid on Tokyo, destroying one square mile of the city. This success was followed on the night of March 9–10, when more than 300 B-29s returned to drop 2,000 tons of incendiaries on the city. The resulting firestorm destroyed 16 square miles, incinerated as many as 100,000 Japanese people, and left a million people homeless in the most destructive attack of the war. The heat was so intense it literally boiled the water in canals.

Through June, continued low-level incendiary attacks on Japan devastated major portions of six large cities. By war's end, 66 cities had been largely reduced to ashes. An estimated 330,000 Japanese, mostly civilians, perished.

The first major Tokyo raid on March 9–10 killed up to 100,000 people and destroyed more than 267,000 buildings—about a quarter of the city's total. Over the next 10 days, B-29s torched a total of 32 square miles in Nagoya, Osaka, and Kobe. Losses among the bomber crews were light. Though some American officers questioned the morality of the attacks, the prevailing view was that the raids were appropriate retribution for Japanese atrocities, would destroy enemy industry, and would demonstrate to the Japanese population that further resistance was futile.

An aerial photo of Tokyo burning. Dissatisfied with the results of high-level bombing, the 20th Bomber Command turned to low-level nighttime incendiary attacks in March 1945.

Very few structures remained standing after the Tokyo incendiary attacks.

"People soaked themselves in the water barrels that stood in front of each house before setting off again. A litter of obstacles blocked their way; telegraph poles and the overhead trolley wires that formed a dense net around Tokyo fell in tangles across streets. In the dense smoke, where the wind was so hot it seared the lungs, people struggled, then burst into flames where they stood. The fiery air was blown down toward the ground and it was often the refugees' feet that began burning first; the men's puttees and the women's trousers caught fire and ignited the rest of their clothing."

–French reporter Robert Guillain, describing a firebomb attack on Tokyo

Werhner Von Braun Surrenders to Allies

Werhner von Braun and his team designed the A-4 ballistic missile, renamed by Josef Goebbels as the *Vergeltungswaffe 2*, the "Vengeance Weapon 2," or V-2. The 46-foot-long, ethanol-and-water-fueled missile could hurl its 2,800-pound warhead some 200 miles. Its highest recorded altitude was 117 miles, making it the first craft to reach outer space. But its guidance system was inaccurate: Chances were about even that it would come within 10 miles of a target.

As World War II in Europe ground to a close in spring 1945, Soviet troops closed to 100 miles of Peenemünde. Most of the V-2 staff decided to surrender to the Western Allies, but in the meantime the SS was ordered to liquidate the rocket engineers and burn their records. With forged documents, Braun and 500 of his staff put together dozens of train cars, as well as about 1,000 automobiles and trucks, and headed toward advancing American troops. At the end of the journey, Braun's brother Magnus buttonholed a GI: "My name is Magnus von Braun. My brother invented the V-2. We want to surrender."

The Americans took Braun and his staff into custody, recovered their hidden records, and seized hundreds of freight loads of V-2 components. Under Operation Paperclip, Braun, his team, their families, caches of scientific records, and enough V-2 components for 100 missiles, were brought to America. Since their Nazi associations would have barred many from visas, the scheme was hush-hush. Stationed at Fort Bliss, Texas, they called themselves "Prisoners of Peace." At the White Sands Proving Grounds in New Mexico, they continued their missile work; progress was rapid. By October 24, 1945, one of their reconstituted V-2s snapped photos from space.

Thereafter, Braun was transformed into an honored, naturalized American citizen, and fulfilled his boyhood dreams. He married his German sweetheart and had three children. In 1950 his group moved to Huntsville, Alabama, and designed the Army's Jupiter ballistic missile, which later launched the first U.S. satellite. He made television programs with Walt Disney that argued for manned space flight. In 1960, in the wake of Sputnik, he was made head of the NASA team that built the Saturn V rocket, which ferried Americans to the moon. He retired in 1972 when NASA opted for the earthbound space shuttle instead of a piloted mission to Mars.

Braun in his office at NASA headquarters in 1970.

Above: A photo of Werhner Von Braun with a broken arm a day after he surrendered himself to American troops.

Right: Werhner Von Braun in front of the F-1 engines of Saturn V's first stage. Speaking to the press after his surrender Braun stated, "We knew that we created a new means of warfare, and the question as to what nation, to what victorious nation we were willing to entrust this brainchild of ours was a moral decision more than anything else. . . We felt that only by surrendering such a weapon to people who are guided by the Bible could such an assurance to the world be best secured."

Fu-Go Balloon Bombs Kill Six in Oregon

By late 1944, the United States had cut off much of Japan's supply of food, fuel, and other war materials. Despite a shortage of resources, the Japanese Ninth Research Division laboratory developed a new weapon. The Japanese knew that a strong wind current swept across the Pacific from Japan to North America (later this current would be called the jet stream). Researchers supposed they could float a large number of missiles on the current to explode over America.

So began project Fu-go. The Japanese decided a hydrogen-filled balloon would be the best method of transportation. Engineers refined the mechanisms to ensure the balloons would be carried along the jet stream at an altitude near 30,000 feet. If they slipped below 30,000 feet, a mechanism would release a pair of sandbags, and the balloons would rise. If they got as high as 38,000 feet, a vent was activated to release some hydrogen from the balloons. Released from northern Honshu, the balloons would take three days to cross the Pacific. With its sandbags spent, a mechanism would drop the bombs and light a fuse that would burn for 84 minutes before detonating a flash bomb that would destroy the balloon.

The first balloons were launched November 3, 1944, and one was spotted two days later off the coast of San Pedro, California. They continued to turn up throughout the northwest United States and western Canada, reaching as far east as Farmington, Michigan and south to northern Mexico. Rather than incite widespread panic, the balloons were largely ineffective and rarely discussed. *Newsweek* ran a report on the weapons in January 1945, and the Office of Censorship issued a notice to the media not to report further incidents.

On May 5, 1945, a minister's wife and children from the Sunday school were on a fishing trip. They discovered a grounded balloon and tried to move it, but it exploded. After this incident, the media ban was lifted so that people could be warned of the potential danger. Researchers examined some of the balloon bombs that were found unexploded and analyzed the sand in the sandbags. Finding that it was not from America or the mid-Pacific, they eventually isolated its origin to the beaches of northeast Japan.

The Japanese government suspended funding for project Fu-Go in April 1945. While Japanese propaganda had declared casualties as high as 10,000, they had no evidence the bombs were actually reaching or exploding in America. In all, of more than 9,000 bombs launched, only about 300 reached the United States.

One pregnant adult, Elsie Mitchel, and five children, Edward Engen, Jay Gifford, Joan Patzke, Dick Patzke, and Sherman Shoemaker, were the unfortunate victims of Japan's balloon offensive.

A photo of a re-inflated balloon that was recovered at sea. An outline of a human next to the balloon was used to give perspective on the balloon's size.

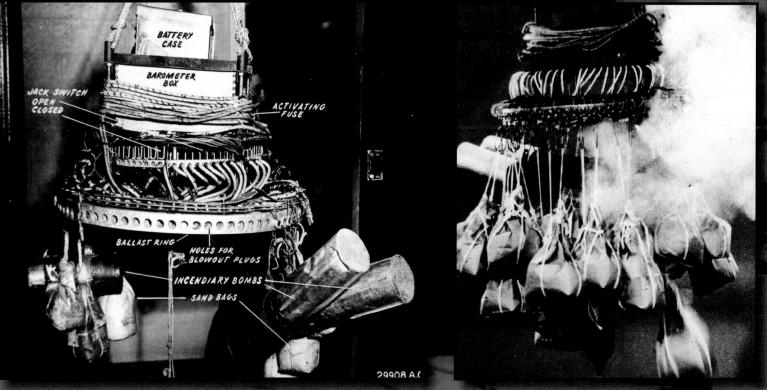

The "brain" of the balloon bomb.

Still from a movie showing ballast release.

The Trinity Test

The development of nuclear weapons began under the umbrella of the Manhattan Project in 1939. Led by Major General Leslie Groves and physicist Robert Oppenheimer, the project began as a small operation that would eventually have a massive effect on the outcome of the war with the bombing of Nagasaki and Hiroshima in August of 1945. The many discoveries in particle physics that occurred throughout the 1930s provided the theoretical framework of such a weapon. But the fear that fascist powers were also trying to create a similar weapon left American leaders with little choice as to whether such a weapon should be made. By the end of the war, the Manhattan Project employed 130,000 people with nearly ninety percent of the project's cost going to the development of nuclear fissile material that would create the weapon's colossal power.

The Trinity Test was the culmination of all the work that was put into the Manhattan Project, detonating the first nuclear weapon, known as the Gadget, in history. The Gadget was detonated in the deserts of New Mexico on July 16th. Talks of whether the test should include the use of a vessel to contain the bomb's explosion were held, and the vessel, known as Jumbo, was delivered to the test site in New Mexico. If used, the bomb would be placed within the vessel and detonated, but the use of the vessel was dismissed because the measurement of the explosion was one of the primary purposes for testing the weapon. Instead Jumbo was placed 800 feet away from the test site on a tower to see if the 150-ton, 15-foot-wide steel cylinder would survive the explosion—it did.

The Gadget was scheduled to be tested at 4:00 a.m., but the test was delayed due to thunder and lightning. The Gadget was detonated at 5:29 a.m., thirty minutes after the rain had subsided. The explosion was the equivalent to 20 kilotons of TNT, which left a crater that was five feet deep and 30 feet in radius. The shockwave from the explosion hit the base camp—located 10 miles from the detonation point—40 seconds after the detonation. The shock of the detonation was felt nearly 100 miles away, and the mushroom cloud that the explosion produced reached nearly eight miles into the sky. The explosion lit the surrounding mountains in such a way that they appeared brighter than day for about two seconds after the detonation with the hues of the illumination turning from purple to green to white. Much of the nuclear fallout remained in the test site, although fallout that condensed into a white mist fell on the Chupadera Mesa some 30 miles away where cattle suffered from beta burns and loss of hair. The effects of the fallout on local citizens in the area are not known due to lack of data. The test was ultimately successful, and the effect that the bomb had would eventually help end the war.

The steel containment vessel, known as Jumbo, being delivered to the test site. Jumbo was originally going to be used in order to contain the bomb's explosion but was later used to test its resilience against the explosion.

The assembled and detonation-ready Gadget sitting atop the test tower with the bomb-assembly leader Norris Bradbury.

A photo capturing the explosion exactly 16 milliseconds after the Gadget's detonation. The explosion's eventual mushroom cloud would rise nearly eight miles into the sky.

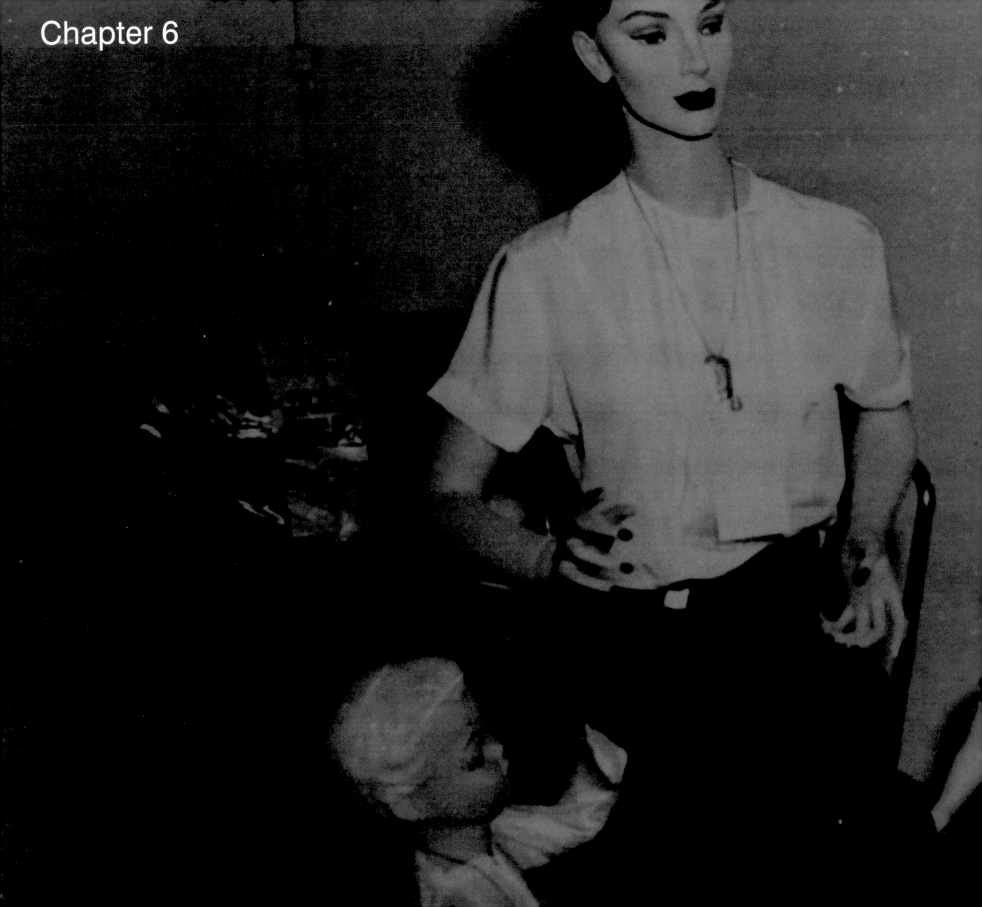

Chapter 6

Forgotten Places

A lien autopsies. Covert military operations. Tests on bizarre aircraft. These are all things rumored to be going on inside Area 51—a top secret location inside the Nevada Test and Training Range (NTTR) about an hour northwest of Las Vegas. Though shrouded in secrecy, some of the history of Area 51 is known. For instance, this desert area was used as a bombing test site during World War II, but no facility existed on the site until 1955. At that time, the area was chosen as the perfect location to develop and test the U-2 spy plane. Originally known as Watertown, it came to be called Area 51 in 1958 when 38,000 acres were designated for military use. The entire area was simply marked "Area 51" on military maps. Today, the facility is rumored to contain approximately 575 square miles. But you won't find it on a map because, officially, it doesn't exist.

The most famous Area 51 employee is someone who may or may not have actually worked there. In the late 1980s, Bob Lazar claimed that he'd worked at the secret facility he referred to as S-4. In addition, Lazar said that he was assigned the task of reverse engineering a recovered spaceship in order to determine how it worked. Lazar had only been at the facility for a short time, but he and his team had progressed to the point where they were test flying the alien spaceship. That's when Lazar made a big mistake. He decided to bring some friends out to Groom Lake Road when he knew the alien craft was being flown. He was caught and subsequently fired.

During his initial interviews with a local TV station, Lazar seemed credible and quite knowledgeable as to the inner workings of Area 51. But when people started trying to verify the information Lazar was giving, not only was it next to impossible to confirm most of his story, his education and employment history could not be verified either. Skeptics immediately proclaimed that Lazar was a fraud.

So what really goes on inside Area 51? One thing we do know is that they work on and test aircraft. Whether they are alien spacecraft or not is still open to debate. Some of the planes worked on and tested at Area 51 include the SR-71 Blackbird and the F-117 Nighthawk stealth fighter. Currently, there are rumors that a craft known only by the codename Aurora is being

Years ago, curiosity seekers could get a good view of the facility by hiking to the top of two nearby mountain peaks known as White Sides and Freedom Ridge. But government officials soon grew weary of people climbing up there and snapping pictures, so in 1995, they seized control of both. Currently, the only way to legally catch a glimpse of the base is to scale 7,913-foot-tall Tikaboo Peak.

An F-22 fighter jet flies over Area 51 during a red flag drill. Groom Lake and the facilities surrounding it can be seen in the background. Getting a clear idea of the size of Area 51, or even a glimpse of the place, is next to impossible.

The main entrance to Area 51 is along Groom Lake Road. Those brave (or foolhardy) souls who have ventured down the road to investigate quickly realize they are being watched. Video cameras and motion sensors are hidden along the road, and signs alert the curious that if they continue any further, they will be entering a military installation, which is illegal "without the written permission of the installation commander."

In 1994, a landmark lawsuit was filed against the U.S. Air Force by five unnamed contractors and the widows of two others. The suit claimed that the contractors had been present at Area 51 when large quantities of "unknown chemicals" were burned in trenches and pits. The suit alleged that two of the contractors died as a result of coming into contact with the fumes of the chemicals, and the five survivors suffered respiratory problems and skin sores. Reporters worldwide jumped on the story, not only because it proved that Area 51 existed but also because the suit was asking for many classified documents to be entered as evidence. Would some of those documents refer to alien beings or spacecraft?

The world would never know because in September 1995, while petitions for the case were still going on, President Bill Clinton signed Presidential Determination No. 95–45, which basically stated that Area 51 was exempt from federal, state, local, and interstate hazardous and solid waste laws. Shortly thereafter, the lawsuit was dismissed due to a lack of evidence, and all attempts at appeals were rejected. In 2002, President George W. Bush renewed Area 51's exemptions, ensuring once and for all that what goes on inside Area 51 stays inside Area 51.

So at the end of the day, we're still left scratching our heads about Area 51. We know it exists and we have some idea of what goes on there, but there is still so much more we don't know. More than likely, we never will know everything, but then again, what fun is a mystery if you know all the answers?

A photograph of Bob Lazar. To this day, Lazar contends that everything he said was factual and that the government deleted all his records in order to set him up and make him look like a fake. Whether or not he's telling the truth, Lazar will be remembered as the man who first brought up the idea that alien spaceships were being experimented on at Area 51.

If you want to try and catch a glimpse of some of these strange craft being tested, you'll need to hang out at the "Black Mailbox" along Highway 375, also known as the Extraterrestrial Highway. It's really nothing more than a mailbox along the side of the road. But as with most things associated with Area 51, nothing is as it sounds, so it should come as no surprise that the "Black Mailbox" is actually white. It belongs to a rancher, who owns the property nearby. Still, this is the spot where people have been known to camp out all night just for a chance to see something strange floating in the night sky.

A little south of Tucson, Arizona, lies the Sonoran Desert, a barren, desolate area where nothing seems to be happening. That's exactly why, during the Cold War, the U.S. government hid an underground Titan Missile silo there.

Inside the missile silo, one of dozens that once littered the area, a Titan 2 Missile could be armed and launched in just under 90 seconds. Until it was finally abandoned in the 1990s, the government manned the silo 24 hours a day, with every member being trained to "turn the key" and launch the missile at a moment's notice. Today, the silo is open to the public as the Titan Missile Museum. Visitors can take a look at one of the few remaining Titan 2 missiles in existence, still sitting on the launch pad (relax, it's been disarmed). Folks with extra dough can also spend the night inside the silo and play the role of one of the crew members assigned to prepare to launch the missile at a moment's notice.

A Titan II missile in a silo ready for launch.

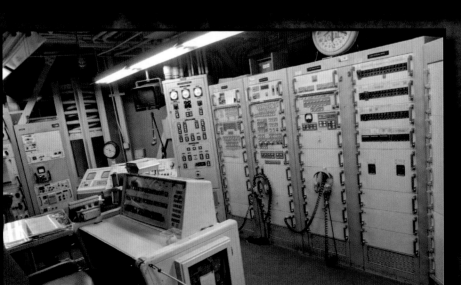

An aerial photo of the 38 remaining Titan II missiles in 2006, waiting to be deconstructed at the Davis-Monthan Air Force Base.

A Titan II missile being test launched at the Vandenberg Air Force Base.

You wouldn't think a sunny place called Peanut Island, located near Palm Beach, Florida, could hold many secrets. Yet in December 1961, the U.S. Navy came to the island on a secret mission to create a fallout shelter for then-President John F. Kennedy and his family. The shelter was completed, but it was never used and was all but forgotten when the Cold War ended. Today, the shelter is maintained by the Palm Beach Maritime Museum, which conducts weekend tours of the space.

An earlier photo of Peanut Island in the Palm Beach Inlet.

A photo of the Port of Palm Beach with Peanut Island seen behind it in the Palm Beach Inlet.

Los Alamos National Laboratory

Until recently, the U.S. government refused to acknowledge the Los Alamos National Laboratory's existence. But in the early 1940s, the lab was created near Los Alamos, New Mexico, to develop the first nuclear weapons in what would become known as the Manhattan Project. Back then, the facility was so top secret it didn't even have a name. It was simply referred to as Site Y. No matter what it was called, the lab produced two nuclear bombs, nicknamed Little Boy and Fat Man—bombs that would be dropped on Hiroshima and Nagasaki, effectively ending World War II. Today, tours of portions of the facility can be arranged through the Lab's Public Affairs Department.

An aerial view of Los Alamos National Laboratory in 1995.

Robert Oppenheimer (right), the laboratory's first director and leader of the Manhattan Project, with his successor Norris Bradbury.

A photo of the Controlled Thermonuclear Research lab in Los Alamos.

Nevada Test Site

If you've ever seen one of those old black-and-white educational films of nuclear bombs being tested, chances are it was filmed at the Nevada Test Site, often referred to as the Most Bombed Place in the World.

Located about an hour north of Las Vegas, the Nevada Test Site was created in 1951 as a secret place for the government to conduct nuclear experiments and tests in an outdoor laboratory that is actually larger than Rhode Island. Out there, scientists blew everything up from mannequins to entire buildings. Those curious to take a peek inside the facility can sign up for a daylong tour. Of course, before they let you set foot on the base, visitors must submit to a background check and sign paperwork promising not to attempt to photograph, videotape, or take soil samples from the site.

American troops watch the mushroom cloud rocket into the sky after a detonation during Operation Desert Rock I in 1951.

A photo from December 17, 1970, of the Baneberry Test where radioactive material leaked from a detonation fissure after a ten kiloton bomb was detonated 900 feet underground. Several dozens of employees